Putting Students First

Putting Students First

A Game Plan for Personalizing Learning

Marsha Jones, Laureen Avery,
and Joseph DiMartino

ROWMAN & LITTLEFIELD
Lanham • Boulder • New York • London

Published by Rowman & Littlefield
A wholly owned subsidiary of The Rowman & Littlefield Publishing Group, Inc.
4501 Forbes Boulevard, Suite 200, Lanham, Maryland 20706
www.rowman.com

6 Tinworth Street, London SE11 5AL, United Kingdom

Copyright © 2020 by Marsha Jones, Laureen Avery, Joseph DiMartino

All rights reserved. No part of this book may be reproduced in any form or by any electronic or mechanical means, including information storage and retrieval systems, without written permission from the publisher, except by a reviewer who may quote passages in a review.

British Library Cataloguing in Publication Information Available

Library of Congress Cataloging-in-Publication Data Available

ISBN: 978-1-4758-5570-8 (cloth)
ISBN: 978-1-4758-5571-5 (pbk.)
ISBN: 978-1-4758-5572-2 (electronic)

Contents

Foreword	vii
Acknowledgments	xi
Introduction	1

PART I: BACKGROUND AND CONTEXT — 5

Michael Robinson's Story (In His Own Words) — 8

1 Putting Students First: Words Matter — 11
   Starting with Personalization — 12
   Supporting Student Voice and Choice — 13
   Balancing Student Agency and Power — 15
   Sharing Leadership — 16
   Defining Success — 17

2 Guided by Theory, Research, and Practitioners — 21
   Learning from Others — 24

3 Professional Agency — 27
   Leadership at the Top Matters — 28
   Everyone Understands the "Why" of Their Work — 29
   Everyone Acts as a Leader — 30
   A Learning Mind-Set — 32
   Adaptive Implementation — 33

4 Sustaining Growth — 37
   Remember What's Important — 39
   Everyone Matters — 39

	Everything Matters	40
	Work Together	40
	Try New Things	40
5	Ensuring Equity and Excellence	41

PART II: THE GAME PLAN — 45

Rules for the Game Plan — 45

6	The Game Plan for Professional Agency	49
	Establish a Leadership Plan	49
	Provide Flexible Schedules	54
	Reflect and Use Feedback to Improve	57
	Connect with Community	61

7	The Game Plan for Student Agency	65
	Provide Voice and Choice for Students	65
	Have Students Ready to Learn	69
	Create Multiple Pathways for Students	71
	Set Goals with Students	75

PART III: IMPLICATIONS — 79

8	Focus on Core Beliefs	83
	Remember What's Important	83
	Everyone Matters	84
	Everything Matters	85
	Work Together	87
	Connect and Network	88
	Try New Things	90

Appendices
  A: Springdale School District Playbook — 93
  B: Personal Learning Plan Sample: Kindergarten — 109
  C: Personal Learning Plan Sample: Grade 1 — 111
  D: Personal Learning Plan Sample: Grade 2 — 113
  E: Student Advisory Program Implementation Survey — 115
  F: Advisory Program Implementation Checklist — 119

Bibliography — 121

About the Authors — 123

Foreword

It is my privilege to write this endorsement for the book titled *Putting Students First* authored by Dr. Marsha Jones with support from Laureen Avery and Joe DiMartino. In every way *Putting Students First* is a great tribute to the teachers and principals of the Springdale school system in Springdale, Arkansas. The Springdale story is, in my mind, a beautiful and professional story of how the Springdale educational team responded to the demographic change in its community over a period of more than two decades.

Springdale is a great city, a great place to live and raise a family. It has always been blessed with great teachers, and the community values its schools and over time has placed the highest priority on service to its youth. In the early 1980s, Springdale was virtually an all white school district, and approximately 13% of the students were eligible for free and reduced lunch prices. The area had a strong agrarian heritage, and it had only begun to grow up economically. Northwest Arkansas had a very inviting appeal—beautiful landscape, clear and abundant water, good schools, available low-income housing, and a wonderful overall quality of life. As economic expansion took root, the opportunities for jobs were plentiful and the people responded—people from all over the world. The immigration had a major impact on both community and school. In those early days, hundreds of families and their children relocated to Springdale, Arkansas. The enrollment increases in the schools ranged from several hundred new students each year to more than a thousand new students annually for a number of years. Today the Springdale School District has an enrollment exceeding 23,000 students in prekindergarten through grade 12. Springdale has become the largest school district in Arkansas.

In addition, the rapid growth in primarily entry-level workers in local manufacturing jobs brought major changes in the socioeconomic levels in the community as a whole and to major ethnic changes in the community. The early immigrant influence was primarily Hispanic and—to a small degree—Asian families moving to the area. Significant changes in the makeup of the community had an immediate impact on the schools. Thus the focus of this new book, *Putting Students First*, is to relate the changes that the local Springdale school system made to address the educational needs of its rapidly growing, diverse, and high-poverty student population in order to appropriately serve its students.

The social change and educational change and the professional changes required in this process were significant—enormous, really. The necessary changes were identified collaboratively by the educational team. A broad course of action was identified, and those new plans were addressed by the entire team. At the heart of the change process was the willingness of the teachers of the Springdale school system to embrace at new levels the teaching and learning of all children. "All" means ALL. The great teachers of Springdale realized that they had to be learners right along with their students. They understood that they had to address language gaps, cultural differences, and significant socioeconomic changes in their students. None of this was easy. In many ways it was "straight up" in terms of the challenges of teaching. Springdale teachers accepted the challenge, just as they had done with special needs children over time. The Springdale culture of placing our children first would accept no less.

Springdale teachers have long realized that the internal accountability system—among all the different versions of accountability systems—is the prime driver of school success. Teachers pursued professional development to learn more about other cultures and the science of cultural transition. They sought English-As-a-Second-Language credentialing and placed additional focus on how to differentiate instruction. They developed models for family literacy that have led to the Springdale School District now having the largest Family Literacy program in the nation.

The humanitarian work of the staff of the Springdale School District created great examples that impacted the city of Springdale, the Northwest Arkansas region of the state, and beyond. In the Springdale schools, it really is all about our students, and the school staff demonstrated their willingness to adjust to meet the changing needs of our students in remarkable and progressive ways. This book, *Putting Students First*, tells important pieces of a story that is still being written. This Springdale team is on an educational journey toward educational excellence that will continue to be written. We understand that education is not a destination; rather, it is a journey.

I believe that the excerpts shared in *Putting Students First* can benefit great teachers and great leaders everywhere. That has always been our hope—that Springdale educators and educators across the country and beyond could learn from our experiences to teach them all ("All" means ALL) and will personalize them to fit their own needs. In so doing they will positively influence the learning opportunities for every student.

I pen these words with great humility and gratitude and with a servant leader's heart as again I say, "Thank you!" to a great educational team—our teachers, our principals, our school board members, and our support staff—for their every effort in pursuing the Springdale School District's mission of teaching them all. It is a great journey, and without question our best work is in front of us!

All of us who have been privileged to be part of "The Springdale Story" welcome your feedback. Collaboration is central to the continued success of our profession.

***Jim D. Rollins, EdD,** Superintendent of Schools*
Springdale School District, Springdale, Arkansas

Acknowledgments

It is essential to extend thanks and credit to the development of the plan for personalization that is represented by the graphic titled "The Game Plan for Personalized Learning" (Figure P.1).

Thinking about how to credit the development of the Game Plan was a challenging task. The Game Plan was not handed to the district on a silver platter, wrapped in a bow with clear definition of giver and receiver. Rather, the key initiatives emerged as we worked together over time to create the system referred to now as "personalization of learning." The graphic became a useful tool when articulating our work in conjunction with the opportunities and requirements placed before us through grant applications and presentations at state and national levels.

To start with, much credit should be given to those pioneers in Pre-K, Darleen Freeman, and Career Academies, Jan Struebing and Kay Mustain who shepherded the process of student centered learning models from concept to reality. Leadership when planning is an inherent requirement of a growing and changing district. Thanks to Dr. Rollins for his unwavering vision. Thanks to my colleagues with the district leadership team, Don Love, Megan Slocum, Shannon Tisher, Jared Cleveland, Mary Bridgforth, Kim Glass, Maribel Childress, Marcia Smith, Kathy Morledge, Hartzell Jones, and external mentors as listed in the narrative, who historically and currently understand how important it is to put students first.

I want to credit and thank the Arkansas Department of Education, specifically Tom Kimbrell, who gave us our very first waiver, allowing the conversation of moving away from the Carnegie Unit to move forward. Credit belongs to our forward-thinking legislators who allow progressive laws to be passed giving schools more opportunities to pursue more personalized systems of learning.

Acknowledgments

A huge "thanks" goes to the amazing Springdale School District faculty and administrators who bravely piloted the concept of advisories, personal learning plans, and student-led conferences, not knowing exactly what to expect; made on-the-spot adjustments; and addressed the quizzical concerns of parents and students. Additionally, it is the faculty who is to be congratulated with their bravery to generate a myriad of learning activities used to stimulate student voice and choice.

Although it was not practical to mention each and every school in the narrative, I know that in each school there have been and are principals and teachers committed to the vision of personalization. Personal thanks goes to the past and current elementary principals: Martha Walker, Bayyari; Michele Hutton, Elmdale; Dr. Annette Freeman, George Elementary; Linda Knapp/Allison Strange, Harp; Michelle Doshier, Hunt; Melissa Fink, Jones; Cindy Covington, Knapp Elementary; Justin Swope, Lee; Maribel Childress, Monitor; Heather Cooper, Parson Hills; Cynthia Voss, Shaw Elementary; Lola Malone/Shelly Poage, Tyson; Kim Simco, Smith; Dr. Regina Stewman, Sonora Elementary; Dondi Frisinger/Lynn Ryan, Walker; and Debbie Flora, Young. A special note in recognition of two schools who very early on demonstrated their vision of personalization through the International Baccalaureate program, Dr. Jerry Rogers/Janet Harris, Westwood Elementary, and Stacey Ferguson, Turnbow Elementary.

Middle school principals who led the way with their advisories and student-centered approaches in the middle school model help shape the model we use in K-12: Susann Buchannan/Stephanie Anderson, Helen Tyson; Alison Byford, Hellstern; Sara Ford, J. O. Kelly; Dr. Martha Dodson, Sonora Middle School.

I appreciate the transformational work of the secondary schools by creating models for others: Dr. Tamekia Brown/ Dr. Todd Loftin, Central Junior High; La Dena Eads, George Junior High; Dr. Michael Shepherd, Lakeside Junior High; Brice Wagner/Audra Lindley, Southwest Junior High; Danny Brackett/ Paul Griep, Har-Ber High School; Pete Joenks/Jason Jones, Springdale High School; Dr. Shawna Lyons/Dr. Coby Davis, Archer Learning Center; Dr. Joe Rollins/Shannon Tisher/Kelly Boortz, Don Tyson School of Innovation.

I am so grateful to the Teachers on Special Assignment (TOSAs), Laura Weiland, Mickey McFetridge, Laura Bishop, Ty Davis, Jennifer Raabe, Janet Harris, Meredith Cox, Rachel Carethers, Leticia Greene, Christy Schrauger, Joanna Eaton, Chelsea Jennings, Linda Odle, and Megan Rojo who helped construct, rewrite, and refine the curriculum and for the teachers who take the curriculum documents and make them tools for authentic student engagement. This is, in many ways, the heart of this work. The energy in the classrooms as students own their work is palpable!

And thanks to our genius data team, Melody Morgan, Albert Crosby, Kelly Hayes, Reta Curtis, and JoAnna Maddox who kept the books so we could track our progress with data that was authentic and accurate. Our technology team, led by Eric Hatch and Alison Byford, who literally built a technology-based classroom from the ground up, were critical to our transformation.

Thanks goes to members of our school board, the Patron Shelf, the chamber of commerce, and our families for opening their minds and hearts to new ways of meeting the growing needs of our schools and our community. Of special note are those school board members who shepherded the process each month the RTTD grant was in effect: Mike Luttrell, Kathy McFetridge, Michelle Cook, Danny Dotson, Randy Hutchinson, Kevin Ownby, and Jeff Williams.

We also know full well that there are many other districts embracing personalization in their own way. Hopefully, by telling our story and by sharing our game plan we can support each other as more and more districts define their own story on the pathway to Putting Students First.

Introduction

One afternoon, in the spring of 1919, my grandfather's home was visited by a group of local townspeople who were in a state of great agitation. "Come quick" they shouted, "those mean boys from the hills have tied up the teacher and run away! Put on your Army uniform, strap on your sidearm, and get to the schoolhouse to retain order!" (Jones 2019)

Storytelling is a long-standing tradition in the Jones family, as is the multi-generational tradition of teaching. When those two elements come together, it can be quite fun! My grandfather told his tale of how he was introduced to teaching. He was the product of a small rural Missouri community with a one-room schoolhouse and itinerant teachers—pretty typical for the area in those days. He was a tall, imposing, handsome young man, especially when dressed to the hilt in his military regalia, a soldier returned from service in the First World War. Early in 1919 he was still contemplating his future when he was "recruited" as a teacher.

Needless to say, my grandfather responded, retained order (without the use of the sidearm!), and fell in love with teaching by building relationships with his students. He went on to have an illustrious career as an elementary principal and a university professor, eventually receiving his doctorate in education. Along the way he instilled a love of education into his four sons, his grandchildren, and great-grandchildren. I am fortunate to belong to this amazing lineage of educators where I learned from my grandfather's wise words and guidance.

I share my grandfather's story with you so you know where *my* early influences came from, and can understand the deep roots education has in my personal and professional lives. I enjoyed the majority of my teaching career in my adopted home of Springdale, located in Northwest Arkansas, deep in the Ozark Mountains. Traditional Ozark culture includes stories passed orally between generations, and so I've chosen to share the Springdale story as a story.

I looked to my own experiences learning and connecting with others as I explored the "secret sauce" in this district, finding my strongest insights emerged when I shared stories of practice and experience with others. It was through listening and questioning that things began to make sense.

This book is divided into three parts. Part I explores the big picture, discusses the theories and research that guided the work, and names some of the ingredients in that "secret sauce." You will not be surprised to find there are NO simple solutions, and that what worked in Springdale may not work *in the same way* anywhere else.

The specific programs and actions, *what we did, and how we did it*, are explored in Part II of this book (the Game Plan). The evidence and results are always front and center, we know *what made a difference*. Personalization, leadership, partnership, empowerment, and collaboration all have starring roles in the Springdale story.

Part III is a reflection on the Springdale approach and takeaway messages for other districts. Can anyone replicate our program? Spoiler alert, the answer is a qualified *no*—because success in your community is going to be different than success in Springdale.

The good news is there are tangible elements that will become the foundation for building and sustaining a culture that will support your own local journey. In short, the Springdale story belongs to Springdale, but there are many lessons to learn that will create and shape new and unique success stories.

Committing to sharing this story with you was not an idea that originated with me. While I was involved on the inside, helping to make the wheels turn, it took partners from inside and outside the district to convince me that we had a story worth sharing. Thus, this narrative is informed by many actors and voices. Coauthors Laureen Avery from the UCLA Graduate School of Education and Joe DiMartino from the Center for Secondary School Redesign (CSSR) are longtime thought partners who convinced me of the potential value of the Springdale story.

In crafting the narrative, we gathered the voices of our district superintendent Dr. Jim Rollins, students, teachers, administrators, and leaders from within Springdale, across Arkansas, and from other areas of the country. These stories complement one another, exemplifying a common belief and vision that students can and should be partners in the learning process. Student ownership of learning is a key ingredient in improved outcomes for our students.

We chose to open this book with Michael Robinson's story. He embodies the spirit of success we want for all our students. We have been on this journey toward student-centeredness for many years, and on the following pages I hope to share some of the lessons we have learned—with a little help from my friends. My hope is that you find the right balance of professional expertise and home-spun advice within these pages. Of course, I hope it also helps you make sense of your own story.

Dr. Marsha Jones

Part I

BACKGROUND AND CONTEXT

> In our Springdale Public Schools, we have established a culture of excellence, a culture of vision and innovation, a culture of inclusion. We are committed to teaching all students to the highest level possible. We are ever mindful that we are preparing our young men and women to live and work in an increasingly complex and challenging global society. With the help of a strongly supportive community of patrons and parents who partner with the schools, we are doing just that. (J. Rollins, Springdale Superintendent Interview, 2019)

Putting Students First tells the story of a large, diverse, public-school district in Northwest Arkansas engaged in creating and sustaining a student-centered educational system.

The Springdale School District is a recognized leader in the nation, and our educators and students continue the district's tradition of striving for excellence in all areas—academics, arts, athletics, and activities. Today, Springdale graduates are broadly successful, outperforming the expectations typically predicted by demography. Recognitions and honors abound, supported by evidence that students are succeeding and thriving.

The Springdale system has been recognized as a "district rising" by Education First, a designation given to school districts where students shattered the predictions for a majority low-income immigrant population. That recognition came even before receiving a prestigious Race to the Top District grant, which catalyzed and accelerated our already substantial accomplishments.

Within the district, the only expectation that really matters is the expectation to keep improving. Improvement and growth are defining characteristics of the students, educators, families, and the wider community. There are unique features of the Springdale culture that contributed to the high levels of success seen in the district, and there is an intentional Springdale way of doing things.

The Springdale School District has been focused on deepening student learning through personalizing learning strategies, supported by a culture of collaboration, for a long time. We think about this as three intertwined strands of work:

- Creating structures within the environment for personalized learning;
- Increasing deep learning through personalization; and
- Building capacity to support and promote personalized learning.

In practice, personalization in Springdale shows up as competency-based approaches, flexible schedules, student-led conferences, personal learning plans, professional learning communities, and many other structures and programs that impact all students, all educators, and the community as a whole.

The speed of growth in the community is staggering, and shows no signs of abatement. In 2000, Springdale had 15 schools and 10,744 students, with 20 percent identified as racial or ethnic minorities. In 2017, the overall student enrollment had more than doubled to 22,771 across 30 schools with 65 percent identifying as minority.

This rapid growth is not simply a matter of numbers and scale. As the numbers grow in Springdale, the educational challenges presented by our newest students become increasingly complex. Our district once had a negligible number of economically disadvantaged students but today reports more than 72 percent of the students as low income. Nearly 40 percent of Springdale's students are English Learners[1] (ELs), with more than half of the incoming kindergarten students meeting that designation. Springdale is now home to more than 3,000 families from the Marshall Islands, making up approximately 11 percent of the student body in our schools, with those numbers continuing to grow rapidly.

Members of the Springdale community would tell you they have achieved success *because* of the growing diversity in their town, not in spite of it. Increasing heterogeneity of the student population creates and propels the need to continually explore and improve pedagogy and wraparound supports. A living example of evolving pedagogy is found in Springdale's approach to supporting the rapidly growing numbers of emergent bilinguals across our community.

Working with emergent bilinguals was a new challenge to the district in the early 2000s, as large numbers of Spanish-speaking families and their children moved into the area. Over the years, the district developed and implemented innovative and successful programs to meet the needs of these students, resulting in significant academic success. Immigration patterns continue to evolve, and Springdale is now also home to a growing community of newcomers from the Marshall Islands.

The emigration from the Marshall Islands is driven by the need for better healthcare and economic opportunity, and the desire for a quality education for their children. Many Marshallese children are not achieving success on par their peers and Springdale educators continue to search for more effective ways of engaging Marshallese students and families. We are finding strategies that worked with the Latino community are not resonating as well with the Marshallese community.

The reasons for this are complex and interrelated with broader social and economic drivers but that has not dissuaded the steady focus and commitment of the schools to make things better by focusing on student achievement while strengthening the roles and relationships among the educators, students, and the Marshallese community.

There was a point in time when we might have gone down a darker path—one that led to student apathy, cultural isolationism, and confusion about our vision and mission. Questions surfaced as our demographics and economics shifted.

Teachers pondered how to reach young students who did not speak English. They were frustrated by their inability to engage with literature when students could not read English novels. Advanced math instruction ground to a halt with students who lacked formal exposure to school and had limited experience with basic computational skills. These were legitimate questions being directed at our leadership team, and in all honesty, we did not have many answers.

I clearly recall the courageous conversations, the student-centered decisions, and deliberate focus and emphasis on *all means all*. This was a stark reminder of the compelling need for continual adaptation and personalization if our district was to survive and thrive in this new world order. Therefore, we set off to find the answers!

In the words of Springdale superintendent Dr. Jim Rollins,

> We could buy into the idea that demography is destiny, but we will not do that. We focus on doing good work, personalizing learning, meeting students where they are, and using gap analyses over and over. All the ideas and "best practices" we uncovered with Latino students and families, like working through faith-based organizations, are not having the same impact with the Marshallese. We pay attention to and keep learning from incremental gains. This is the same process we used with our Latino sub-population, but we are exploring different strategies and moving towards new outcomes. (Rollins 2019)

The storyline in Springdale is always the same. You hear and see empathy, kindness, and support. There is an honest commitment to always putting students first. Educators, family members, and community partners are well-read with every action informed by learning theory and educational research. No one ever believes they are done, and everyone wants to keep getting better and learning more. There is an unshakeable faith that every problem has a solution if you are willing to work toward finding it.

Before we leave this section on background and context, I want to introduce you to Michael Robinson. Michael graduated from Springdale High School in 2010, and went on to successfully matriculate from Brown University in 2014. He is currently a doctoral candidate at the Harvard University School of Divinity. Michael's story and context as a student and his inspirational success remind us what happens when we *Put Students First.*

MICHAEL ROBINSON'S STORY (IN HIS OWN WORDS)

From the late 1990s until the time I graduated in 2010, I had the privilege of being a student of the Springdale School District. The historical backdrop through which my classmates and I navigated consisted of a community wrestling with its identity during drastic social change.

In the wake of explosive population growth, combined with a radical shift in racial demographics, a once white-majority school district transformed into a white-minority district with skyrocketing enrollment almost overnight. Northwest Arkansas' low cost of living, combined with a surplus of both white- and blue-collar employment opportunities, made it an attractive option for immigrants seeking a better life and for resettling individuals in the aftermath of Hurricane Katrina in 2005. Suddenly, teachers and administrators had to address, with urgency, questions of how to accommodate all of these new students and teach in cross-cultural contexts, often with significant language barriers.

I imagine one of the hardest parts about being a teacher is that you are never quite sure what your lasting impact is going to be. Each year you start with a collection of strangers staring back at you that you hope to aid in learning, and by the end of the year you have one or more classes of students you have taught—each with their own unique personality—that are the outcome of your yearlong triumphs and persistence through setbacks.

Along the way the hearts and minds behind the students' faces grow more visible as they become a consistent part of your daily life and you theirs. However, the end of the year comes inevitably and these students who you have journeyed with and even come to love are gone. If I were a teacher I would wonder: Where did my students end up? Do they remember me? Did my work matter and make a difference in their lives?

What I can say about Springdale School District is that its work mattered and changed my life. As a black, mixed-race student I contributed to the destabilization of the racial homogeneity of Springdale's student population, and with also coming from a low-income, single-parent home benefited from the district's success working through how to personalize its teaching, programs, and services. This community came together and decided that they would not let education be defined as simply an impersonal presentation of curriculum but as a transformative relationship that required attention to the multidimensional lived realities and identities that students bring with them into the classroom.

Putting Students First is intended to illuminate and draw lessons from this moment in Springdale's history when its school district had to make critical decisions on how it was going to respond to change and, if it was going to accept it, how to make it work for every student and not just some. Fortunately, I was the product of a school district that decided without hesitation that demographics should not determine destiny.

While every student who thrived through Springdale's work undoubtedly has a different story and set of relationships that defined their experience, what defined mine were teachers who took a special interest in me and made me feel that I mattered by developing programs and creating spaces meant to foster positive involvement. I wish this for every student. I will never forget the school libraries and bookmobiles that my teachers and principals ran during the summer to make sure I had the newest releases of my favorite book series. I'll never forget the band and choir directors that arrived early and stayed late to open their rooms giving me somewhere to belong while I practiced and grew friendships.

I'll never forget the teachers who took on extra work to run the International Baccalaureate program, and researched summer and scholarship opportunities to present during class. Even today, I am only able to tie my tie because my principal taught me how. Springdale School District took me in and instilled in me counter-narratives to combat the many that exist in every community that tell students their present reality is what they should accept as their life's trajectory. I would not be who I am today without them as they pushed me to have dreams greater than the ones I had for myself.

What continues to speak volumes about Springdale's success is not only the role it played in my life but the impact it has had among my classmates. It is amazing to see so many friends, especially those from similar underrepresented backgrounds, choose to dedicate their lives to being educators and specifically seek to return to Springdale School District. Those students who first walked through Springdale School District's halls in the midst of immense social change twenty years ago grew up and are now the next generation asking questions on how to design, implement, and sustain the necessary programs and cultural shifts to ensure that every student has the opportunity to succeed. These teachers have been grafted into a teaching community who continue to push forward in building Springdale School District's legacy.

Educators give their lives away one school year at a time and piece by piece to each of the students they have. Even though teachers may never see some of their students again after having taught them, every moment with a student is an opportunity to have a profound influence on a life that is just beginning. *Putting Students First* asks you to join Springdale School District with your own unique vision for your community to help pave the way for future students who will go on to do things no one can yet imagine.

If a community really does strive to put students first, there is no doubt that they will look back in the future and wonder: Where are my teachers now? Do they remember me? Do they know how much their work mattered and how much of a difference it made in my life?

NOTE

1. The term "English Learner" is used in reference to the classification system used by the State of Arkansas. Throughout this text we use the term "emergent bilingual" when referring to children in the Springdale Schools who are acquiring the English language. The term "emergent bilingual" refers to a child's potential in developing bilingualism; it does not suggest a limitation or problem in comparison to those who speak English.

Chapter 1

Putting Students First

Words Matter

Our teachers are all working to make their classrooms more innovative and to empower students to own their learning. We have reached a point where we are allowing students to learn from a menu—and that's exciting and empowering. Now it's time for us to move from the menu and become short-order cooks for our students. That part of our journey is going to require having a variety of ingredients in our pantry, a variety of utensils and appliances in our kitchen, and mostly lots of energy for cooking!" (Childress 2019)

The local paper in Springdale runs a weekly column sharing interesting peculiarities of the English language. By reading the weekly column you might learn that words can be altered by common usage to upend their original intent. An example of this is the word *peruse*—originally meant to read thoroughly, it now also means to scan, based on popular usage.

In the same way, the language used to talk about education can be particularly confounding, and we ran head first into this while working on telling this story. Our big goal as storytellers was to construct a narrative around an emerging teaching and learning model where students are viewed as partners in the learning process, as opposed to simply being vessels into which knowledge is poured. In our own conversations, the phrases "student-centered learning," "personalization," "student voice and choice," and "student agency" kept popping up, used interchangeably. There was always the implied tagline—"you know what I mean." Or "you know it when you see it."

But words matter, and we found that clarity in the terms used strongly supports clarity and focus in our actions. If we want you to understand our story, we need to be precise in describing the foundational elements and the words used to talk about it.

STARTING WITH PERSONALIZATION

"Personalization" describes ways the adults create the conditions for change in an educational system—teachers move from providers of content to coaches and supporters of learning. Early in our journey, we knew with certainty that success with increasingly diverse learners called for a shift to more nimble and skilled educators who could sustain classrooms designed around the needs of students. We eventually adopted the elements and definition of *personalized learning* developed by Barbara Bray and Kathleen McClaskey (2014) included as figure 1.1.

Bray and McClaskey title their chart as "Personalization vs. Differentiation vs. Individualization." As educators, we were very familiar with the expectation to differentiate and individualize our instruction based on the needs of the students. We had been trained by the very best with the excellent resources provided by experts in the field, such as Tomlinson's *The Differentiated Classroom* (1999).

Our *ah-ha* moment came when researching the definition of "personalization" as our inquiries led us to the work of Bray and McClaskey. They have captured the differences in a clear and concise way—differentiation and individualization are what the teacher is doing to support the student. Personalization is what the student is doing to engage in the learning process.

Differentiation and individualization are important as we create the conditions for optimal learning. As educators we have a responsibility to attend to the learning needs of our students. However, if the student does not engage, actively participate, and own the learning process, the work of the educator may not have a lasting impact. The Bray and McClaskey descriptors helped define what those behaviors look like as we explore innovative ways of unlocking the student's own capacity to direct their learning, monitor progress toward meeting goals, and find relevance in the learning outcomes.

This is not the only way to define *personalization*, but it was the way that spoke most clearly to Springdale educators. In literature and common usage, we find that this term (*personalized learning*) is frequently defined in terms of the technologies used to support it, the implication being technology can improve instruction in ways that personalize learning. But here in Springdale we have always been more invested in defining personalization in ways that related to learning.

The Bray and McClaskey model that guides so much of our work defines personalization in terms of learners, stressing student ownership, and responsibility for learning. The Bray and McClaskey chart became a powerful tool used to measure all initiatives and strategies, and determine if they were helping us move toward a personalized system. It was not uncommon to see this chart come out during discussions to help decide if any particular action truly fell into the personalization column and was thus worth promoting.

Personalization vs. Differentiation vs. Individualization Chart (v.3)

There is a difference between personalization, differentiation, and individualization. One is learner-centered; the others are teacher-centered.

Personalization	Differentiation	Individualization
The Learner...	**The Teacher...**	**The Teacher...**
drives their learning.	provides instruction to groups of learners.	provides instruction to an individual learner.
connects learning with interests, talents, passions, and aspirations.	adjusts learning needs for groups of learners.	accommodates learning needs for the individual learner.
actively participates in the design of their learning.	designs instruction based on the learning needs of different groups of learners.	customizes instruction based on the learning needs of the individual learner.
owns and is responsible for their learning that includes their voice and choice on how and what they learn.	is responsible for a variety of instruction for different groups of learners.	is responsible for modifying instruction based on the needs of the individual learner.
identifies goals for their learning plan and benchmarks as they progress along their learning path with guidance from teacher.	identifies the same objectives for different groups of learners as they do for the whole class.	identifies the same objectives for all learners with specific objectives for individuals who receive one-on-one support.
acquires the skills to select and use the appropriate technology and resources to support and enhance their learning.	selects technology and resources to support the learning needs of different groups of learners.	selects technology and resources to support the learning needs of the individual learner.
builds a network of peers, experts, and teachers to guide and support their learning.	supports groups of learners who are reliant on them for their learning.	understands the individual learner is dependent on them to support their learning.
demonstrates mastery of content in a competency-based system.	monitors learning based on Carnegie unit (seat time) and grade level.	monitors learning based on Carnegie unit (seat time) and grade level.
becomes a self-directed, expert learner who monitors progress and reflects on learning based on mastery of content and skills.	uses data and assessments to modify instruction for groups of learners and provides feedback to individual learners to advance learning.	uses data and assessments to measure progress of what the individual learner learned and did not learn to decide next steps in their learning.
Assessment **AS** and **FOR** Learning with minimal **OF** Learning	Assessment **OF** and **FOR** Learning	Assessment **OF** Learning

Personalization v Differentiation v Individualization Chart (v3) by Barbara Bray & Kathleen McClaskey
Version 3 is licensed under a Creative CommonsAttribution-NonCommercial-NoDerivs 3.0 Unported License
Download chart at http://tinyurl.com/yd8ma99x and website for any updates: kathleenmcclaskey.com/toolkit
For permission to distribute copies, contact Kathleen McClaskey at khmcclaskey@gmail.com

Figure 1.1 Personalization versus Differentiation versus Individualization. Bray and McClaskey, 2014.

SUPPORTING STUDENT VOICE AND CHOICE

By definition (at least by our definition), personalization requires changes in student behaviors and attitudes. Learners in personalized systems actively participate in and drive their own learning. This ability for a student to take responsibility and manage his or her own learning is often referred to as "student voice and choice." The ability to manage your own learning can have significant effects on academic achievement and personal growth.

Student voice and choice have accelerated the development of creative, engaging, and rigorous work in the classroom. For example, a group of female students at the Don Tyson School of Innovation were interested in learning about drones, and created a program to explore the related math and science principles, taking advantage of a Springdale program that promotes problem-based, science, technology, engineering and math (STEM) learning. But these young women wanted to go further and engage younger girls in the project.

Coding Takes Flight has engaged over 1,000 elementary school girls from across the district. Abby Herrera, one of the student developers, said, "I really love seeing the young learners get excited about things . . . it's really fun to see them be like, 'yeah, I can do this. It's not just my older brother who can do it'" (Arkansas Online News 2019).

The female high school students in this example were able to experience the relevance of math and science to an emerging career pathway while transferring their excitement to a younger generation of girls. What made this program particularly impactful is the positive role models the older girls provided for the younger girls. In a district such as Springdale, where poverty levels are high, experiences such as this offer equitable enrichment experiences in ways that are not typically supported by the traditional curriculum.

This example is voice and choice in action. Students are taking control of their learning, building on their passion, and transferring the learning to a real-life application—while at the same time ensuring that relevant educational outcomes are being achieved.

> Since the move to personalization in our classrooms, students are aware of their actions as a learning. They are not only aware of their academic standings, but also of their qualities that make them/will make them a better learner. (K. Johnson 2019)

Students taking ownership of and responsibility for their own learning is nearly universally accepted as a desirous and positive trait. When students have a say in what and how they engage with content, learning deepens and carries over into new applications and areas. There are numerous, well-documented and research-based practices designed to support and promote "student voice and choice," including things like project-based learning, student involvement in school governance, and advisory programs where individuals set and work toward short- and long-term goals.

Today Springdale embraces and widely supports pathways to increase student voice and choice. In our way of thinking, voice and choice provide freedom for students to select a path to a particular outcome. We see success when we allow students to select how they will learn core content.

Increasing voice and choice almost universally leads to improved student engagement, deeper learning, and more successful outcomes. The complexity of our classrooms, socially, emotionally, economically, and academically, is more than one teacher and even a team of teachers can accomplish—without help! The help comes from the students themselves when conditions are created so that they get excited about our chosen content, curriculum, and activities.

BALANCING STUDENT AGENCY AND POWER

Agency is a subtly different, though related, concept. Again, the words and expressions that we commonly use in education often imply very different meanings to different people. *Agency* in education relates to the expression of free will and power, and would be reflected in the freedom of a student who chooses *what to learn*. *Agency* is a popular term lately, and many educators talk about increasing student agency as an ultimate goal. But in Springdale we believe a thoughtful balance of agency and power between teachers and students is a key strategy for success.

> Why does it matter if you have voice and are given choices in school? Having options helps me learn better, it helps me be prepared for when I am grown up. (Student 2018, JB Hunt Elementary)

Springdale's Don Tyson School of Innovation has given us the chance to pilot a program that offers students a considerable amount of autonomy and *agency*. During the early years of this program, when student numbers were small, individuals had tremendous leeway in *how* they learned. Within very broad parameters, students also had the freedom to select *what* they learned. As the numbers grew and this innovative program scaled up, we found we needed to scale back on some of the student autonomy and agency as we looked for that "just right" balance.

Today, even the most innovative settings in Springdale align their content to district-adopted standards, albeit with flexible approaches to instruction and curriculum. This is not a backslide, or a reversion to the old way of doing things. Instead, it represents deliberate attempts to strike the right balance between teacher and student agency and power. As with everything else we do, we believe this balance is constantly shifting and it will change from school to school, from teacher to teacher, and from student to student.

SHARING LEADERSHIP

Sharing leadership with students was one of the hardest challenges Springdale Schools faced as we moved ever closer to *Putting Students First*. Joe DiMartino, president of the CSSR, pointed out that "in order to better serve students, schools must create a set of conditions in which students are empowered to become key partners in the decision–making process about issues that affect their daily experiences in school" (2019). When Joe DiMartino and CSSR came to work with us in 2015, his first order of business was to visit with students.

At the time this seemed a curious request, but we honored it, trusting in his thinking. He went on to challenge our view of the world by suggesting the most important change process for a school district was to compel students to become more engaged partners in the process of schooling.

One way to do this is to allow students to lead their own learning conferences. Instead of the traditional "parent-teacher" conference, his suggestion was to let the students in on the conversation—after all, they can and should contribute. People were a bit skeptical at first, but a few pioneers led the way, starting at the elementary and middle schools. The reaction was amazing, with first-year data indicating 90 percent of parents supported this new approach. Teachers were impressed with how well students responded as they rose to the occasion well-prepared to share their own stories. Instituting these student-led conferences across all schools, with all students, turned out to be a powerful lynchpin for change in Springdale.

Sharing leadership, power, and agency does not imply that instruction is compromised. There is always a place for direct instruction, use of challenging text-based reading, and accountability for learning within clearly defined standards. Rather, it implies the teacher helps design and support activities for students that attract them, draw them in, hold them, and fasten their attention. Students need to have a clear understanding of what they are expected to know and be able to do. In order to do that, teachers need to know their students—their aspirations, their interests, their ideas. Hence the success of the *Putting Students First* approach.

DEFINING SUCCESS

By all rights, folks interested in the story of Springdale should ask *why we consider ourselves a success*. A simple question, with a very complex set of answers. Reflecting on this question made me recall the parable about blind men and an elephant. The man touching the side of the elephant might describe it as a wall. But the one holding its tail would tell you it was a rope. In the same way, describing success often depends on which part of the elephant you are in contact with.

Parents, students, community members, local and state boards of education, professional organizations at the state and national level—everyone has their own methods of acknowledging success. As a high school parent, you may want to brag because your high school student received the prestigious National Merit Scholarship, or because they earned agriculture honors at the Washington County Fair, or because they played on the Springdale High School state championship soccer team.

Students from George Junior High can brag on their achievement as state winners in the Samsung for Tomorrow contest—they earned a $20,000 award and are competing for national recognition. Springdale students at Hellstern Middle School and Young Elementary School look forward to the trip to Ames, Iowa with their "Odyssey of the Mind" (OM) team, having successfully made the cut to compete in the OM World Finals.

The community is justifiably proud when teachers and administrators are selected as State Teachers of the Year or Administrators of the Year. Springdale educators, including teachers, counselors, and administrators from every level, have been honored by their peers from across the state for outstanding work. Community bragging rights are in order when the district is one of only fifteen communities across the United States presented with the All-American City Award from the National Civic League for an innovative reading initiative. Organizations entrusted with funds to invest in the community, such as the United Way of Northwest Arkansas, think highly enough of the Springdale School District to invest in a summer reading program, providing $200,000 in resources over the next two years.

A quick look at Springdale's Annual Report to the Public (Springdale Public Schools 2018) highlights the many ways that students are recognized for success. What is so impressive about the report is the sheer volume of student-driven references. Students are celebrated in each and every school, across a multitude of personal and team accomplishments, community engagement activities, challenging academic competitions, and enrichment activities.

Of course, as educators we look to the data and metrics used to mark academic success. A look at how our students are growing academically is a meaningful measure of our own growth. Are we meeting the needs of each child? Are we challenging our emergent bilingual students and those with gaps in their learning?

The University of Arkansas Office of Education Policy created a metric for determining how students were improving from one year to the next based on the ACT Aspire (ACT, Inc. 2012) assessment. While Springdale educators use many assessments and measures, we find the ACT Aspire growth scores to be particularly insightful because they are designed as longitudinal measures aligned with college and career readiness benchmarks.

> NCLB was supposed to result in all students being proficient by 2014—it required 100% of students to reach the same standards. What went wrong? Maybe our reliance on standardized assessments isn't the best way to define success. For example, in Massachusetts postsecondary success rates are significantly higher than their test-based proficiency scores would predict. Obviously, we need to explore different ways of defining student success. (DiMartino 2019)

The Office of Education Policy recognizes certain schools for "Beating the Odds." These are high-poverty schools where the growth of their students is greater than expected. In 2017 Springdale had eight high-poverty elementary schools and two high-poverty junior high schools recognized for making better than expected growth gains for their students. An additional four schools, not considered schools in poverty, were recognized for excellence in overall growth of students.

Positive impacts on culture and student engagement are observable. The number of students with chronic absence and out-of-school suspension has decreased significantly. More students are completing college and career readiness activities like senior exhibitions. Overall graduation rates have increased significantly from 82 percent to 87 percent, with the largest increase among African American (77 percent to 86 percent) and Hispanic students (79 percent to 87 percent). These rates are not where we want them to be, certainly, but we are making steady progress.

The CSSR helped schools complete the Traditional/Transitional/Trans formational Survey (2014) in 2014 and again at the end of 2016. The results of the survey were overwhelmingly positive and indicative of significant growth. Teachers and administrators note they see an increase in student ability to set (and meet) personal and academic goals. Professional development is designed to give teachers time to practice, with coaches working alongside them. Technology and live streaming are being used to share information and learning across the district. At all levels there is a sense of autonomy coupled with accountability.

We are not suggesting that the definition of success implies that all goals are met or that any one piece of the work is perfected. That would be a foolish proposition giving the ever-changing disposition of school—students grow and change year to year; political winds change with elections and legislative sessions; innovations are improved upon or discarded over time. All of these elements keep educators constantly striving to adapt and change while keeping a clear sense of vision and mission.

An example of a bold, new, and successful enterprise for our students is Springdale's Don Tyson School of Innovation. Superintendent Dr. Rollins addressed the graduates and reminded them,

> You have created something great. A new school, a new model of education, a school devoted to personalized learning, anytime, anyplace, any pace learning, one that is engaging, one that is relevant, one that is rigorous, one that assures that each of you has a voice in your school experience. One in which you have become more and more in charge of your own learning. We understand the potential and promise that you represent. We are excited about the influence that you will have and the contributions that you will make. (Rollins, Speech to First Graduating Class, Don Tyson School of Innovation 2019)

Defining success is tricky and the metrics of success are even trickier. What we really want is to see our students grow and mature into contributing members of our world. The statistic and the measures change at a whim—what doesn't change is our responsibility to encourage and support our students in personalized ways so they can maximize their potential. That is the driver behind the initiative we call *Putting Students First*.

Chapter 2

Guided by Theory, Research, and Practitioners

> These are our ancestors. We explicitly stand on their shoulders. (Jones 2019)

We constantly talk about change and innovation in education, and the truth is we are *always* moving, learning, and adjusting course. The rapid growth in population and the diversity of challenges brought to Springdale may have compelled us to move faster than others. But most school districts have an inherent desire to improve, compelled by the moral imperative to meet the complex needs of our students.

We bought into change but needed new ideas that held the promise and potential of helping us achieve our goal of engagement for each student. We understood we were learners and sought out "experts" to guide and inform our journey. Early on, we settled into an explicit way of operating—trial and error.

As educators we are exposed to hundreds of "silver bullets" if not more, that tell us "if only we would do such and such" miraculous learning will occur. We listened, read, and visited to learn as much as we could. We explored, adopted, and adapted many programs, strategies, and practices. We walked away from some ideas as well. Inevitably we experienced differing levels of success as we tested out new ways of educating students. And in the midst of it all, we kept moving closer to our end goal—get a complex mixture of students on a path to high achievement.

Our journey toward student-centeredness, and our own growth from novice to competence in this area, has been enabled by the support, guidance, and expertise offered by others along the way. Our "gurus" include seminal thinkers in multiple fields as well as teachers, students, and others we were fortunate enough to meet along the way. We seek to understand, explore, and adapt elements from these individuals, weaving them into the tapestry that becomes the Springdale story.

An important thread in the Springdale story is the widespread and deep understanding of educational research, theory, and practice. People understand the "why" of things and freely debate the relevance of promoted practices. However, there is a historic lineage of thinkers and doers in the field that have a large and lasting impact on the Springdale community—researchers and writers that we have returned to over and over.

Seven Correlates of Effectiveness (Edmonds 1979) (Lezotte and Snyder 2010)

- Clearly stated and focused mission
- Instructional leadership by all administrators and staff members
- Opportunity to learn
- Safe and orderly environment for learning
- Climate of high expectations for success
- Positive home-school relations
- Frequent monitoring of student progress

This district-wide embrace of commonly held core principles is unusual—it does not waver with changes in leadership or follow the prevailing winds of change. It is broadly and deeply rooted, maintained through constant reflection as theories are translated and shaped into practices.

The Springdale community can trace the philosophical and practical foundations of our beliefs to the groundbreaking work of educational researchers emerging more than forty years ago, particularly Ronald Edmonds (1979) and Larry Lezotte (2010). Although it seems self-evident now, they were pioneers in establishing correlations between the attributes of school and student success. Together they described seven Correlates of Effective Schools: leadership, mission, climate, high expectations, monitoring of student progress, family involvement, and opportunities to learn. These correlates remain the bedrock of all work done in Springdale to date.

The 1980s and 1990s brought a wealth of theorists and educational activists focused on redesigning the high school experience. The Springdale Schools were early partners and students of the work done by Ted Sizer and his Coalition of Essential Schools (2013); we were early adopters and piloted the Coalition's Essential Principles at one of our high schools. Superintendent Dr. Rollins reflects back on this time: "In the early years we all read Horace's Compromise (1984). It made a lot of sense to me, and when things make sense to you to gravitate towards them. You also attract people who feel the same way. So, we read, and we talked about things, and we began to attract people who felt the same way" (Rollins 2019).

This experiment did not survive in its original form in Springdale, but collegial conversations around building student-centered schools as core principles have evolved and are still evident in the structure of our secondary schools today. Another lasting influence on Springdale is Rick Dufour (Dufour and Eaker, Professional Learning Communities at Work: Best Practices for Enhancing Student Achievement 1998), who introduced us to Professional Learning Communities (PLCs) and helped structure and extend collegial, learning-focused discussion to all levels. PLCs and collaborative teams are endemic in all our schools and the mechanism that makes everything else work.

Changing the roles and relationships between students and teachers is one of the basic shifts toward a student-centered learning environment. Doug Fisher and Nancy Frey provided us with a practical and reasonable approach through their framework for what they call the "Gradual Release of Responsibility" (2014). Fisher and Frey provided a systematic way for students to begin to own their learning. They affirmed sound instruction, based on focused lessons, direct instruction, modeling, collaborative learning, checking for understanding, and ultimately an independent exhibition of the learning.

> All learning is essentially independent learning. That is not to say that teachers don't play a profound role in students' learning. It just means that we must ultimately ensure that students take responsibility for their learning. We can do this through the materials we provide, the supports and scaffolds we offer, and the feedback we communicate to our students. (Fisher and Frey 2014, 27)

Fisher and Frey also recognize that student choice can, and should, be part of the equation. They encouraged the faculty to be more flexible in their assignments in order to promote student demonstration of learning. This was done through the concept of independent learning tasks that are meaningful, experiential, and relevant. Students are encouraged to use their reading, writing, and research skills to focus on topics that interest them. Ultimately responsibility for learning is released to the student.

When it came to conceptualizing and implementing programs, the work of Barbara Bray and Kathleen McClaskey (2014) was extremely helpful. In particular, we frequently went back to their distinctions between personalization, differentiation, and individualization (discussed in more detail in chapter 1). In a field rife with confusing terms and implications, district leaders used their definitions to help keep everyone on the student-centered path.

LEARNING FROM OTHERS

The decision and practice of *Putting Students First* in Springdale really illuminated the value of learning from our peers, those practitioners who were pioneers in personalizing learning. Given our limited experience with student-centered learning we sought out schools and districts who were already engaged in implementing interesting practices. We started with schools and districts in New England, based on the recommendation of Joe DiMartino and the CSSR.

During our journey to New England, we had a great opportunity to see practices in place that would help Springdale Schools move the needle toward personalization of learning. Halldale High School (Hallowell, Maine) gave us the chance to engage with a community that had implemented and embraced competency-based learning. Souhegan High School (Amherst, New Hampshire) served as an exemplar of strategies to support and sustain student agency. At the Francis Parker Charter Essential School (Devens, Massachusetts) we saw ways in which innovative performance assessments could be used to engage students in demonstrations of learning.

The Nashua (New Hampshire) high schools welcomed our group from Springdale, along with other professional colleagues *and* students from the region. While we visited, observed and engaged in conversation with administrators, teachers, and students, the host schools were gathering insight into their own progress in personalizing learning. These visits afforded Springdale Schools the opportunity to join a true learning community where the strengths of the journey were celebrated and the areas of challenge were shared with supportive next steps.

It was an amazing opportunity to witness the insights and wisdom of both adults and students as guests and hosts interacted with each other. We took home a plethora of great ideas for content but equally valuable were the process takeaways. It was comforting and empowering to understand that we were all on the same journey, and learning together.

We learned a great deal about technology from others. While our Springdale community was changing socially, economically, and ethnically, the world in which we lived had also changed to a place where seamless technology supported everything we did.

Online shopping, banking, and technology-enabled communication, we were living a "new normal." As educators we were immigrants in this new world of technology, and had a long list of arguments against implementing technology in the classroom. You have certainly heard these arguments. This would work if only . . . every student had a computer, every teacher knew how to integrate computers in the classroom, every school had access to the internet, and every device was affordable and durable.

> Students at East Pointe Elementary in Greenwood, Arkansas, develop personal leadership skills. As one student said, "Find your voice and inspire others to find theirs." Greenwood's hallways are filled with examples of student-driven interests: robotics, drama, art, recycling. Students speak enthusiastically about their contributions and involvement with school activities. At East Pointe, eight kindergarten teachers were working with an instructional facilitator to build a common assessment item, tied to a specific learning standard. Several sample assessments were shared and consensus built around the best fit. Teachers then explored ways to ensure consistency in administering the assessment. Teachers brainstormed ways to keep the rest of the class engaged while administering this individual task (Ray 2019).
>
> East Pointe Elementary in Greenwood, Arkansas, is rural district near the border with Oklahoma. The school has been identified as a "PLC at Work" school by the Arkansas Department of Education.

However, thanks to the support and guidance from many of our peers in and outside of education, we began exploring places where technology was already working. We networked, explored, and found ways to get around the barriers. Today Springdale is a district of 1:1 technology, with affordable Wi-Fi and a cadre of well-trained teachers integrating technology in meaningful ways. Students can attend school physically, virtually, or through a personalized blending of the two.

The learning momentum has not stopped. We cannot overemphasize the value of learning from and with peers. These days, we host our own site visitors and always learn as much from our guests as they might take away from us. Theorists, researchers, and practitioners continue to explore the complex, powerful relationships between personalization, student-centered learning, and student success—and we continue to read and learn from them. As leaders in this emerging movement we remain avid students, hungry to learn and share as widely as possible.

Chapter 3

Professional Agency

Whenever hard decisions or dilemmas arose, we always asked the question, "What is in the best interests of the child?" (J. Rollins, Springdale Superintendent Interview 2019)

Colleagues frequently ask about "leadership" in Springdale, and what fostered the amazing shifts in practice from a traditional school environment to one that prioritizes student-centeredness and personalization of learning for students.

Leadership theorists will tell you the vision for any organization needs to be nurtured at the top—and Springdale's superintendent, Dr. Jim Rollins, has always had a clear and unwavering vision about the purpose of education and the role schools play in that vision. Our district is unique in that our superintendent has been in the district for more than forty years, and there is definitely a positive impact when the right leader is at the helm for a long time.

Yet we know that the leadership impact extends beyond the superintendent's office. Springdale is full of leaders at all levels possessing a sustained, deliberate, intentional focus on leading change.

Our journey toward personalization was not kicked into action by a new buzzword or an opportunity for targeted grant funding. The journey began with the focused and clear expectation that every child was expected to succeed—and accountability among the educators for that outcome. To help in our journey we found like-minded experts who broadened our thinking and brought research-based strategies that expanded our capacity to meet the needs of all students. Allowing children to sit in classrooms where failure is rampant is against the nature of what it means to be an educator—it is our moral responsibility to ensure success for all.

The work in Springdale has helped us to gradually build a culture that supports the individual success of each student. Sharing models of engaged, student-centered classrooms helped reinforce the message that *Teach Them All* was both practical and attainable in our own classrooms. Standards and mastery learning, project-based learning, engagement versus compliance in learning, problem-based learning, and the gradual release of responsibility model were all components leading to an authentic model of personalization of learning for children. We were building our airplane as we were flying.

LEADERSHIP AT THE TOP MATTERS

Dr. Rollins's professional belief system was formed and influenced by the Effective Schools movement during the 1980s. This work has stood the test of time and legitimately sustains the "Putting Students First" model even today. His leadership posture is often summed up by a foundational mantra—*Teach Them All*—that has come to define the entire community. Rollins's passion for achieving this goal is actualized through his high, explicit expectations for students, staff, and community members. His focus was on equity—not just equality.

Students who are immigrants or living in poverty often face barriers that must be addressed before students can access what is available to them. All students are eligible for special enrichment programs, but can all families afford the fees and extra cost? All families are welcome in the school, but do all families understand the system of schooling in the United States? All students are invited to participate in school sponsors' activities, but do language barriers keep a family from attending?

As a leader, Rollins would challenge his staff to look beyond equal opportunities afforded to students and see the hidden barriers that may be keeping a student from maximizing their potential. In other words, we need to make sure that opportunities are equitable, not just equal.

One of the benefits of a rapidly growing school system is the ability to hire new administrators who share a common vision. As central office staff and building-level principals were brought into the system, the initial interview process focused on discussions around the principles of Effective Schools and the strong belief that every child has the right and capacity to be successful. During the interview process it was made clear that this was a shared responsibility. Principals, in turn, hired teachers and staff with the same expectations. In Springdale finding people with common beliefs who cared deeply for children and their success is a foundational element of our success.

EVERYONE UNDERSTANDS THE "WHY" OF THEIR WORK

> All organizations start with WHY, but only the great ones keep their WHY clear year after year. What if the next time someone pushes, "What makes you better than your competition?" we answer with confidence, because the work we are doing now is better than the work we were doing six month ago. And the work we're doing six months from now will be better than the work we're doing today. Because we wake up every day with a sense of WHY we come to work. We come to work to inspire people to do the things that inspire them. (Sinek 2009, 224)

In the early 2000s a new era was emerging in the field of education. Public schools were highly criticized, charter schools were being funded as a solution to the failure of traditional public education, and technology was coming forward promoting anytime, anyplace learning. At the same time, our traditional school district was growing rapidly with vastly shifting demographics. Immigrant students were pouring into the district at the rate of 800 to 1,000 per year.

Writing a book "after the fact" is an exercise in recollection and hindsight. We have spent countless hours discussing and dissecting "leadership." Everyone acknowledges there is a systemic culture that puts students' needs first. Springdale insiders and outsiders agree there is something special here, though naming and describing it has been more challenging. Many of the elements tied to the transformation of practice were triggered by a common understanding of vision and mission shared by the people within the Springdale School District. We understand why we do what we do.

The mantra *Teach Them All* is the foundation for the belief system of the district, based on the Correlates of Effective Schools. These principles, which bring hope to even the most difficult learning situations, have served as guideposts in Springdale for more than forty years. *Teach Them All* is consistently emphasized by the school board, administration, faculty, students, families, and patrons. When visitors come to the district to look at our programs, at any school, any level, they walk away knowing what we believe in. There is a pervasive and shared understanding that our work is focused on student growth and success for each, despite vast background differences.

Serious conversations about the future of Springdale Schools continually looked at, and pushed, the status quo. Unsurprisingly these conversations focused on supporting students with increasingly diverse and complex needs. But they also talked about the future of Springdale Schools in an increasingly competitive economic environment and the related reality of maintaining the trust and confidence of families in the community.

Throughout these months and years of courageous conversations, the tenets of Springdale Schools held fast. The commitment to excellence and support touched all students and families, even in the face of harsh pushback. The WHY of the district, *Teach Them All,* and the resulting *Learning for ALL* applied to students who came to school "from across the street or across the ocean" as Dr. Rollins was fond of saying, "when they reach our doors they are one thing . . . they are ours." Everyone, at every level, at every school understands the WHY of their work.

EVERYONE ACTS AS A LEADER

When everyone shares the passion about the students, everyone owns the agenda leading to personalization of learning. Everyone leads the change. The literature on leadership provides example after example that leadership is a group activity. The idea that a single individual or closed group can be credited with great accomplishments is not realistic.

> In the thousands of cases we've studied, we've yet to encounter single example of extraordinary achievement that didn't involve the active participation and support of many people. (Kouzes and Posner 2003, 22)

Broad involvement and inclusion, and yes, leadership, are woven throughout the Springdale story. We find leadership in Marshallese and Latino families who engage for their children despite language and cultural barriers. Community and teaching and support staff leaders with powerful voices have emerged through involvement in the superintendent's cabinet.

A special focus on teachers as leader is at the heart of the collaborative nature of the district. At the building level, teams of teachers work together in grade-level PLCs to analyze student achievement data, create common assessments, and brainstorm instructional approaches and supports. Building-level PLCs are the *key leadership structures* mediating ideas into practice, as well as the key conduit for feedback for improvement.

For example, the district developed a Teachers-on-Special-Assignment (TOSA) model where content experts with current classroom experience work to support the design of standards-aligned curriculum. The TOSAs work collaboratively with building-level professional learning communities to implement and adapt curriculum as needed. The result is a common, high-level approach to curriculum that looks slightly different in each school as it is adapted to the unique needs at each site. These ongoing efforts to match programming to evolving student needs are *only* possible when leadership is distributed, and decision-making is empowered at levels closest to the classroom and students.

Teacher leadership occurs in the development of curriculum. Once the initial curriculum writing had been completed, teams of teachers using the documents provided valuable feedback. Ongoing tweaks in the curriculum documents allow for improvements in the formative assessments, changes in the number and types of learning activities, the addition of new student resources, and recommended instructional strategies. Our experience has found that the best curriculum work involves those best equipped to create functional documents—our faculty members!

The leadership qualities that families bring to the mix is also a major part of the Springdale story, and are often the key to community and political support. We benefit from families who believe in and support our schools for a variety of social, financial, and cultural reasons. We benefit from families who value education and reinforce the teaching and learning process. And we need all families represented.

Our district has been blessed with a very supportive community with active parent/teacher groups and energetic fundraising booster groups. One unique tool that supports the family voice in leadership is the *Patron Shelf* of the superintendent's cabinet. Each month, families, PTA leaders, administrators, and district-level staff meet for approximately two hours in order to share common interests and concerns. The Patron Shelf also serves as a critical two-way communication channel, especially important when major changes are proposed or implemented. Time spent with our community and family members has proven to be a key link to keeping the district moving forward together.

Springdale has also established a Family Literacy program, and developing community leaders among immigrants and lesser-heard voices is an explicit outcome of the work. This model offers English language courses in the school, during the day, where participants explicitly practice their English while role-playing ways to interact with the school. The impact we are seeing for our families is tremendous. The important role of family and community members in supporting our schools during a period of transition can never be overstated. We need all our families to understand the WHY of our work and help us navigate the ways in which we could best serve all our students.

Other examples of teacher leadership take place in the context of what we labeled "Joint Council." Representatives from each school building meet monthly with district-level leadership to consider issues of the day that directly affect the areas of curriculum and instruction. Representatives are given importance and timely district-level information and discuss topics placed on the agenda by the faculty members. Processing changes in policy that affect curriculum and instruction, suggestions for professional development, and sharing of success stories are routinely part of the monthly agendas. This model complements the Superintendent's Patron Shelf as a method of direct feedback and communication between school faculty and the district office.

A LEARNING MIND-SET

Early on, our leadership team began to engage in design thinking and adaptive modeling. Elements of design thinking begin with asking "what if" questions. What if we could get waivers from some of the rules? What if we could have more flexibility about how and when students come to school? What if we placed equal focus on academic content *and* applied learning opportunities? What if we brought the community into school to enhance the learning experience?

Springdale's expansion of early childhood education stemmed directly from this type of disruptive approach. Several years back, kindergarten teachers across the district were overwhelmed with underprepared children coming to their classrooms, many not speaking a word of English. It was a stretch to start thinking and talking about Pre-Kindergarten (Pre-K) education, when public education in Springdale had *always* begun with kindergarten at age five or six. But *what if we embraced the concept of having three- and four-year-olds at school?*

Once the question was asked, we immersed ourselves in learning about Pre-K education. We sought funding and grants, retrofitted buildings, and hired leaders, administrators, and teachers who were skilled in the area of Pre-K. *Teach Them All* now extends to three- and four-year-olds and Springdale now has the largest Pre-K program in Arkansas.

We began to thoughtfully challenge the traditional way of doing school. Our leadership team embraced the tenets of design thinking: understand and have empathy for students who want an alternative school experience, start the thinking process with questions, look at all the possibilities, embrace ambiguity when solutions are not obvious, understand that implementation can be messy, act sooner rather than later, and seek input from many sources. One concrete outgrowth of this approach was the creation of a school of innovation, a place where we could pilot and experiment with new models and approaches.

Today the Don Tyson School of Innovation has grown from 150 students in grades 9 and 10 to 1,230 students in grades 6–12 and is viewed as a demonstration model for the state. Additionally, three other Springdale Schools have been designated by the Arkansas Department of Education as "Schools of Innovation": Westwood Elementary, Turnbow Elementary and Sonora

Middle School. As a result these schools have more flexibility in scheduling and programming.

ADAPTIVE IMPLEMENTATION

When we began our journey toward *Putting Students First*, very little had been documented on personalized learning as a way to improve the teaching and learning experiences for a very diverse population of students. We had a well-defined goal but no clear roadmap of how to get there. We adopted an *adaptive, learning mind-set* to help guide us through this work because we expected to learn and change things during the implementation process. Adaptive implementation and design thinking provided systematic frameworks for collaboration as we tuned, adapted, improved, and scaled deeper learning strategies.

The Springdale School System is an organic, evolving, learning, and growing ecosystem—an *adaptive system*. Embodying an adaptive approach and way of thinking (*adaptive implementation*) drives this ongoing, never-ending search for improvement. In important ways, adaptive implementation-based systems contradict the prevailing wisdom in education that all best practices can be documented and replicated with success.

The movement to require adoption of research or evidence-based practices rests on a powerful but implied assumption—success on a small scale can be copied and should lead to wider use (scaling up or diffusion of practice). We have a strong desire to believe that what happens in the lab can be replicated at scale in the field. If your implementation experiences are anything like ours, you consistently run into challenges that require you to either adapt or abandon your journey.

As we gained confidence in our work, we gradually moved away from the idea of trying to replicate best practices "with fidelity" and found better results in modifying and adapting practices to fit the Springdale context. This approach acknowledges that adaptations are always necessary to find the best fit and results. In the same way, what is working in Springdale will not work in exactly the same way in other schools.

> Teaching is not rocket science. It is, in fact, harder! A NASA rocket scientist turned math teacher said that. Why? Because rocket science involves parts and systems that function exactly as designed, but education is far more complex, dynamic, and interesting. In technical systems you can reliably predict outcomes. But adaptive systems learn and grow, relying on professional knowledge and experience to tweak and improve implementation. (Yamaguchi, et al. 2017, 3–4)

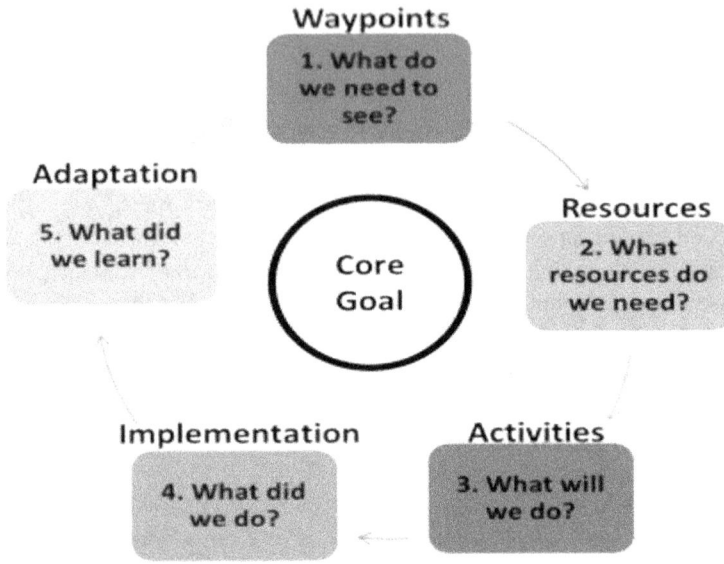

Figure 3.1   Adaptive Implementation Cycle. Yamaguchi et al., 2017.

Practitioners are rarely interested in scaling up or diffusion. Their concern is with implementation on-site—be it in their classroom, school, or district. They are more interested in "scaling down" in the sense that educators want to learn how to make programs work and fit in their local context, with their students.

Springdale adopted the adaptive implementation (Yamaguchi, et al. 2017) approach (see figure 3.1) to guide our improvement process and apply design-engineering principles to the work of improving education. We expect to redesign elements of the program each year, and set aside time to do this. Using this systematic framework ensures there is ongoing attention to activities and impacts, with the need for adjustments and improvements anticipated.

Essential questions are part of our review process including the following: *Did we do what we said we were going to do? What worked? What didn't work? How do we know? What will we do differently? Are we trying to scale up or scale down? Should we keep doing what we have been doing?* This review and planning process establishes important timelines, responsibility for tasks, and a calendar for the next review process.

Feedback on program design, team progress, teacher and student outcomes is collected throughout the year, sometimes with the specific assistance and guidance of our research and evaluation partners through surveys, interviews, data review, and observations. Informal feedback is frequently collected and shared between teachers, coaches, administrators, and others.

Leadership relies on these feedback data to make informed decisions. Formal surveys, interviews, anecdotal evidence, and documents provided by internal and external sources created a strong, uninterrupted flow of information. When something was not going as planned, we heard about it and we took immediate action to fix it. We collected quarterly reports from staff members who were engaged in newly implemented innovative practices. They set their work goals and reported on their progress. As work progressed, internal accountability became firmly entrenched and the external accountability became less and less necessary.

An important foundational aspect of cultures where adaptive implementation can take root and flourish is being open to change. This is more than a question of being flexible as individuals, and it is more fundamental than a willingness to "embrace change" or "think outside of the box." It is much more about honesty in looking at the entrenched constraints. Educational systems are locked in place by implicit and explicit structures that limit the ability to change, adapt, and ultimately to learn. Adaptive cultures, like Springdale, name and examine the elements that work against change and take care to make *putting students first* the *only* fixed, nonnegotiable element in their ecosystem.

Chapter 4

Sustaining Growth

> If there were a silver bullet, I would be using it. So, I have to be smart about taking the best of what works and applying it to my practice. Classroom teachers need to take pacing guides and curriculum plans and adjust them. We need to tweak them in order to align more closely with what our students are focusing on in their classrooms, to add additional goals, to modify for emergent bilingual parents, and to make them "friendly" in ways that allow my students to read and explain their own learning goals. (Childress 2019)

Springdale School District has created a highly personalized approach to learning that is generating successful outcomes. This alone is worth studying and celebrating. But a more startling trend is clear: Springdale is sustaining these positive outcomes while continuing to learn and grow.

In a field characterized by the revolving leadership door, the forty-plus-year tenure of Springdale superintendent Dr. Rollins is remarkable. It is an easy leap to tie that longevity to sustainability. Of course, having a strong leader with a clear vision at the helm for so many years is a major factor. But there are other factors in play as well.

As discussed earlier, the focus on personalization began a long time ago. Though it is hard to pinpoint precisely, ideas began surfacing nearly two decades ago when the population in Springdale began to rapidly grow and diversify. Educators were faced with a choice—they could stay the course and blame the "newcomers" for failing scores, or they could find new, inclusive paths and move forward together. Dr. Rollins is often credited with taking the leadership at this point and advocating for a *"Teach Them All"* approach, though he himself would tell you he successfully channeled and captured the spirit and wishes of the community.

Springdale was exceedingly fortunate to receive a prestigious Race to the Top District award from the US Department of Education in 2013. This grant was awarded, in part, in recognition of the work already underway across the district. But there is no doubt that the infusion of funding and national support accelerated our progress. In the same way, this grant provided an opportunity to take stock of the impact of personalizing learning in our district through a partnership with an objective evaluator.

As the grant funding ended in 2018, evaluators noted the following (Avery and Cervone 2017):

- Positive impacts on culture and student engagement are observable. The number of students with chronic absences and out-of-school suspensions has decreased significantly.
- More students are completing college and career readiness activities like senior exhibitions.
- Student academic growth has been documented through a variety of measures.
- Family, students, and staff surveys show there has been steady growth in embracing and supporting the elements of personalization.
- Teachers and administrators note they see an increase in student ability to set (and meet) personal and academic goals.
- At all levels there is a sense of autonomy coupled with accountability.

Although the signature Race to the Top District grant funding has ended, everyone involved in or touched by the work agrees that the work is far from over. Though focused on a common goal (personalization), every school, every grade level, and every teacher had the support needed to shape implementation in ways that worked for their community. For example, initiatives like student-led conferencing are now embedded in every school, but the process for preparing and conducting them varies by site. This variety is not viewed as an aberration but instead as a rich repository of learned adaptations.

As we look back and reflect on *how* and *why* Springdale has been so successful in sustaining our work, we keep coming back to the notion of culture. Our culture supports and nurtures this work. The culture that allowed and encouraged us to innovate and experiment is the same culture that allows us to sustain our journey.

We have distilled five essential ingredients in our "secret sauce" that were key to our success—and we think they will be key to your success as well.

1. REMEMBER WHAT'S IMPORTANT

"Yes, we can do that" echoes across the Springdale halls and classrooms, and that attitude has everything to do with our ongoing success. In Springdale the message has been consistent, and the focus has always been on the student. Everyone looks at education as a moral imperative, and letting demographics determine destiny is just not an acceptable cultural norm.

First and foremost, the district has demonstrably shifted our culture toward personalization and has developed structures and procedures to support and sustain that change. *Putting Students First* is a vision embraced by the community; it is an integral part of how the Springdale educational family views itself. Community members are taken aback when you ask them if the vision might change when there are shifts in the members of the leadership team at the district or building level. People note changing the personalization vision would be akin to losing high school football. Both are sustained through love and passion within the community.

To effectively close gaps we all thought about the social, emotional, mental, and physical health of the child. Wellness clinics were established in high need areas. As we began to look more intentionally at the whole child, our *teach them all* mantra expanded to include *and reach them all*. Children were arriving from distant places with difficult pasts—but our focus did not change—every child was to be successful—using all available resources. Administrators and community partners understood the moral imperative of this expectation and worked hard to ensure that faculty members were supported in the work.

2. EVERYONE MATTERS

Caring for the teachers and educators who make this happen every day is another cultural norm, and it is so enculturated in Springdale that people hardly notice it. Yet if you look back on other school redesign efforts they are often marked by failure resulting from lack of support, infighting, and jealousy among staff. *Teach them all* applies to every adult working or volunteering in Springdale as well. Professional knowledge is respected and nurtured, and teachers are empowered to manage their own personalized learning journeys. These core principles are explicitly woven into onboarding for new staff. After an initial building period we find educators who share these beliefs self-select Springdale as the place they want to be.

3. EVERYTHING MATTERS

Personalization has somehow come to be associated with high school redesign, as though students are not mature enough to guide their own learning before that time. We know that is untrue, and that Springdale has amazing experiences with personalized approaches even at the Pre-K level. In addition, trying to change a student's perception of school after eight years is really, really hard. "Everything" encompassed every grade level. Every initiative was planned with PK-12 in mind.

4. WORK TOGETHER

Professional learning communities are everywhere in Springdale, and great effort is made to ensure that all staff belong to at least one. Many people are members of multiple groups. Early on the community recognized that there was no "right" way to organize these communities so structurally they look and work differently. But every meeting starts with "why are we here" type questions. What are we doing today? How can we support our children? How can we help our children grow?

5. TRY NEW THINGS

The tradition of continuous learning for educators is evident in the Springdale School District. But more than that—there is a culture that supports and embraces positive change where student welfare is concerned.

For example, Springdale established the Don Tyson School of Innovation as a place to innovate and experiment. The Don Tyson School of Innovation is a lab school for the district; it's a place where we can field test ideas before moving them out. Staff and students self-select to attend this particular high school to minimize the "shock effect" of innovative practices. The other schools in the district that have since been designated as schools of innovation (Westwood Elementary, Turnbow Elementary, and Sonora Middle School) serve as laboratories for unique programming for their students. As a result, they now serve as pilot and demonstration sites and share their experiences with others.

Throughout the years we have been intentional in gathering strategies and approaches that work well in our schools and consistently produce positive change. In Part II we offer you the Springdale *Game Plan* and invite you to learn about the details of this work—what we think is important and how we sustain the elements we find most useful.

Chapter 5

Ensuring Equity and Excellence

> Hope seemed to be a key part to my dreams and just as important as the coursework was for me to learn. I also needed people who were willing to teach me what hope meant. (Robinson 2016)

In Springdale, we support personalization as a pathway to equity. Experience clearly showed us that differentiation and individualization alone *were insufficient* for creating conditions that foster authentic engagement for every student. Personalization isn't a program. In Springdale it is the story of working toward a more equitable process of learning through building on the strengths and interests of our students by working in partnership with all community members.

Although the concept of equity is grounded in elements of program and practice, Michael Robinson's quote taken from a "back to school" presentation at Har-Ber High School, really spoke volumes about the heart of equity. Michael was invited to Har-Ber as a former graduate (2010) to share his inspirational message of overcoming social and academic adversity with the support of and encouragement of his teachers. All academic doors were open to him. But as he said in his speech to the faculty, "From the teachers I've gotten to speak with, hope also seemed to be a common thread. Hope that through education, students would discover that they are capable of more than they ever imagined and can reach their full potential. Teachers that define success that way, changed my life" (Robinson 2016).

The catalyst for hope is found within the nuts and bolts of practice that create the conditions for students to reach their full potential. Several key programs and practices are provided in the narrative as examples. The district's English as a Second Language (ESL) program is considered a model program, offering daily, integrated language instruction to all students. All teachers have been well trained in current best practice models for teaching literacy and math skills in ways that are effective for emergent bilinguals.

The district has sophisticated multifaceted plans for engaging families, with nationally recognized programs like the Springdale Family Literacy program and a volunteer program for men known as Watch D.O.G.S. (Dads of Great Students). Both programs bring families into the school to become part of the school culture. The Family Literacy program builds knowledge and skills for the academics at school, including English language instruction. The Watch D.O.G.S. program provides for an extra set of eyes and ears on the grounds of the school before, during, and after school when dads volunteer to be on-site at their child's school a few hours per month.

Engagement is encouraged through lots of formal and informal gatherings for families throughout the school year sponsored by the schools, booster clubs, and the parent/teacher organization.

When families are new to a community and unfamiliar with local culture, it is essential that *extra* steps are taken to support engagement. For example, we routinely translated notices about special school events into Spanish or Marshallese, but we also needed to make sure the translations were communicating as intended. Sending home reminders about "open house" caused some of our newly arrived families to scratch their heads and wonder why we were opening the windows and doors to the school on one specific night. This experience, and others, heightened our awareness to the intended and received messages embedded in communication.

When written invitations are not sufficient for a parent response to attend a "back to school" event, fall carnival, or student-led conferences, home visits are in order. Face-to-face communication goes a long way in building trust. Offering a friendly smile by the principal and counselor along with a personal invitation to attend is a great tool for getting reluctant parents to school.

Communication challenges also arose as part of student-led conferences. We found that students and families needed support with the academic language used to define the standards, assessments, and learning targets discussed at these meetings. In order to assist students and families we called for bilingual community volunteers and offered a workshop focused on the expectations and language of student-led conferencing. We were very happy (and somewhat surprised!) that in exchange for a light supper, we secured amazing community partners who were willing and able to help our families and our students have meaningful conversations.

For us to become increasingly culturally responsive, we needed help from those who were more experienced with insight and research. We specifically benefited from individuals at the University of Arkansas ESL department, beginning with the work of Dr. Margaret Clark and her experiences with second language programming. Dr. Diana Gonzales Worthen has been instrumental, and helped secure grant funding to establish our Family Literacy program and several additional grants training faculty (certified and noncertified) on how to provide academic support for children in the ESL program.

District staff built a comprehensive program based on informed advice from local and national experts. New positions were created, new assessments were developed, and new models of instruction were introduced. The goal was always to determine the best plan of action for our newcomers and their families. Their work also included finding and providing resources that helped teachers and administrators create culturally responsive classrooms.

The district made a unique hiring decision and hired a well-known local Latino personality, Al Lopez, to serve as an official community liaison. Lopez and Dr. Diana Worthen cofounded One Community Arkansas (One Community 2009), an organization dedicated to bringing people together to improve health, education, and leadership skill. Originally from Puerto Rico, Lopez used his musical talent and local radio show to bridge communications between the school and Latino community.

Helping families know when school was closed due to inclement weather, or special teacher professional development days, or explaining the "chain of command" to solve problems are examples of the messages and topics he covered on the radio. Later Al began hosting a local television program featuring district leadership—putting faces and names together in multilingual and multicultural conversations.

Working with the Marshallese community required different kinds of partnerships. Special meetings were held with the church leaders and the community leaders in order to build trust and understanding. Dr. Rollins found that the Marshallese community would engage more freely when they had their own time to meet with school leaders. Thus, a Marshallese Patron Shelf meeting was established to meet one time per month. The response has been outstanding—sixty to eighty members of the community choose to attend each time.

This is a dramatic increase in participation when only four to six members of the community would attend the traditional Patron Shelf. The extra effort has paid off with stronger communication channels now in place with a once reluctant group of patrons.

We recognize that offering quality programming does not guarantee all students will participate and engage, thus we consistently and explicitly explore the questions of engagement of all students. Effectively and efficiently sustaining equity with a diverse population of students is an ongoing task.

We have noticed places within the district that exemplify equity. Most notably the Springdale High School Career Academies, as well as district programs in athletics and the arts. We found students were excelling in these programs regardless of their socioeconomic background or their primary language and were committed to success. These programs were capturing the spirit of personalization through equity. Advanced Placement classes, International Baccalaureate programs, dual enrollment classes, advanced-level math classes, enrollment in internships, EAST project-based learning classrooms, enrollments in gifted and talented programs, and the Don Tyson School of Innovation all demonstrate a demographically balanced roster of students.

We do not look for equity simply through academic lenses. Pictures of students participating in football, basketball, band, choir, and robotics reveal students from all sectors of our school community.

What is the key to these examples? These successful programs match students with their interests, passions, and skills. Student participation makes a difference. When you are in a real-world internship at a hospital, the relevance and importance of what you are learning is easy to grasp. You are constantly being challenged to do your best and achieve your goals because the rest of the team is depending upon you. Your performance matters.

But students are not alone in their pursuit. Extra tutoring by selfless faculty members before, during, and after class, extra time provided to students as needed to meet the learning targets, access to online tutoring for anytime, anyplace practice are all part of the support system. "You can do this and I will help you" is heard over and over as teachers counsel their students.

An important takeaway about creating equity is the need to think outside the box of traditional practice. We have shared some examples of what we did and what are doing now to work toward a more equitable school environment. What never changes is the need to engage in a learning mind-set that puts the interests of all students at the center of decision-making.

These qualities of equity and excellence motivate us to find ways to expand the type of impact these programs were having on each and every student—not just the privileged few. That really is this intended purpose of this narrative—we want to share our story with the hope that others will be motivated to do the same—to find those models that move us closer to equity. The synergy that comes when students and their teachers share common goals leading to successful outcomes is a story that can be told many ways and under many circumstances.

Part II

THE GAME PLAN

As you begin to plan out and implement your program, you need to think through the potential steps in your journey. Just as in chess, you choose your first move by considering the array of possible subsequent moves. (Yamaguchi, et al. 2017)

RULES FOR THE GAME PLAN

- Develop and consistently restate the commitment to the success of all children
- Permeate the district with like-minded leadership
- Provide access to Best Practice experts
- Establish a whole child culture that surrounds each student with support
- Establish distributed leadership systems that encourage best practices to be adapted to the needs of each building
- Use a design process when looking at innovation
- Face the reality that it is difficult to lead something you do not understand
- Expect to stretch
- Gather evidence
- Realize that giving voice and choice to students is the real test of personalization of learning

In Part 1 of this book, former Springdale High. School student Michael Robinson (class of 2010) commented that the school district "had to make critical decisions on how it was going to respond to change and, if it was going to accept it, how to make it work for every student." In an effort to harness and understand the multifaceted, transformative shifts in Springdale, to document and learn from those critical decisions, we developed the Springdale Game Plan (Springdale Public Schools 2017)

This pictorial representation (figure P.1) shows the interconnected elements that formed the basis for our success with personalized learning.

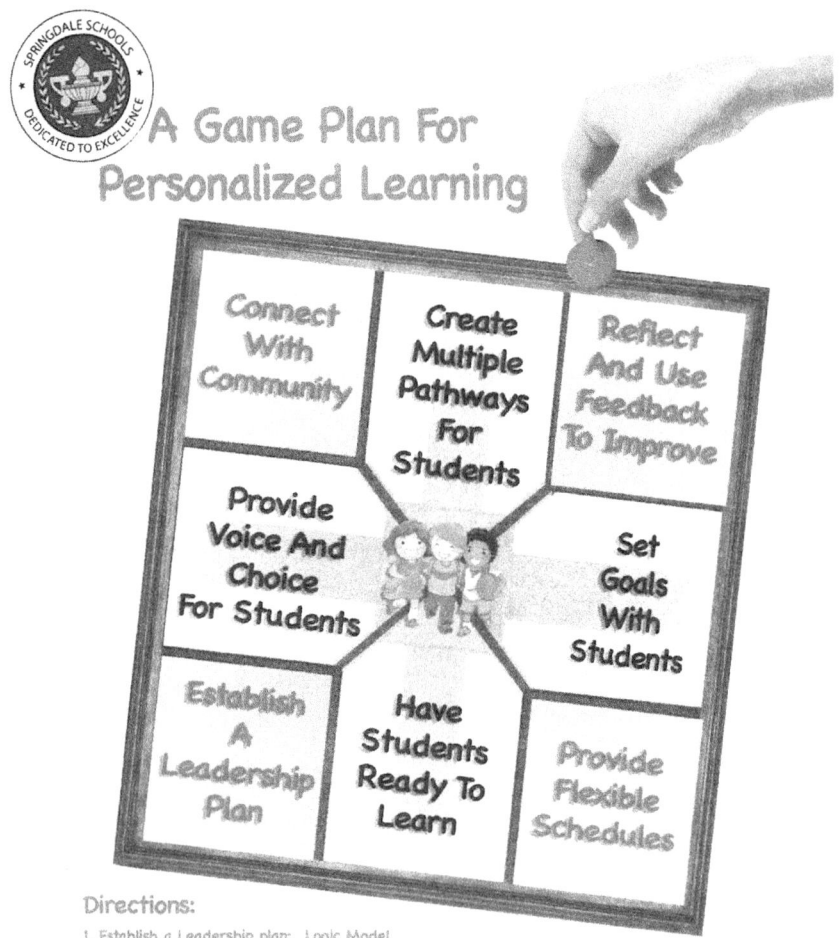

Directions:
1. Establish a Leadership plan: Logic Model
2. Have students ready to learn: PreK
3. Set goals with students: Personal Learning Plans/Student Led Conferences
4. Provide flexible schedules: Seat Time Waiver/ Revised Schedule
5. Provide voice and choice: Advisory/ Technology/ Highly Qualified Professional Development
6. Connect with Community: Parent Involvement
7 Create Multiple Pathways: Academies, School of Innovation
8 . Reflect and use feedback to improve: Professional learning communities; coaching and evaluation

Figure P.1 Springdale Game Plan for Personalized Learning. Springdale Public Schools, 2017.

The way the pieces fit together began to emerge after years of work as we began to reflect on our own transformation. Each component started as an independent strategy, initiative, or practice. We built our Game Plan piece by piece—keeping some, refining others, and discarding still others along the way.

We started by looking at various personalization practices and said, "let's try that" or "that seems like something we should do with our students." We put those practices into the mix as distinct projects to be carried out as we began the transition into a personalized learning model. It wasn't until we were well into the process that we began to understand the relationships among projects.

Light bulbs turned on as we made connections. It quickly became clear a siloed, single project approach was not the way to success. Everything was connected to everything else.

For example, we soon discovered that goal setting with students cannot occur unless we have systematic data collection systems built into the curriculum. Advisory is more meaningful when students have personal targets to meet based on their own data. Understanding data and setting goals with students require time during the school day via an advisory period. Motivation to set goals increases when students have a real audience and use their own voice during student-led conferences.

True to the belief system of the district, the Game Plan places students at the center of our work leading to personalization of learning. Surrounding the students are eight components that we found to be central to accomplishing our goals. We have roughly divided them into two categories—those that directly act on *professional agency* and those that directly act on *student agency*. The reality is that these are tightly coupled initiatives, interdependent activities that rely on both student and adult agency to take effect. This graphic provides a good platform for presentation and discussion as we continue to share and deepen our understanding of what it takes to make *Putting Students First* a reality.

Our thinking about the components and how they are defined evolved, and it is likely it will continue to change. We have moved away from conceptualizing components as "student" or "adult" initiatives and now think more about empowering all players in the system. Individual components may have *more* of an influence on one group than another, but everyone has a role to play in implementing and sustaining them.

You can see the evolution clearly in the *Connect with the Community* component. Initially, this component reflected a family engagement project designed to bring immigrant families into the school setting during the school day. While we were building this project, we were also discovering that our project-based learning models, giving students choice and voice in learning, opened the floodgate to new community connections. Students at Walker Elementary created a community garden in partnership with a local grocery store and a national food industry association. A student project at George Junior High used Geographic Information System mapping techniques and discovered our county ranks as one of the lowest in the state for childhood influenza vaccinations.

In practice, when we stepped back and let each component take on a life of its own, really interesting things started to happen. We stopped trying to define, and instead moved toward describing. When we are willing to enable more and more student voice and choice amazing and unpredictable outcomes will follow.

The takeaway is that when making system-wide changes, there will be many facets of change. Creating some type of graphic can be of great help in making sense of the change practices that are required. This graphic provides a good platform for presentation and discussion as we continue to share and deepen our understanding of the value of personalization of learning and what it takes to make it happen.

Springdale's Game Plan evolved over many years of concentrated effort to formally redefine district practice, showcasing the sustained changes in practice. The development was led by teachers, administrators, and staff members. A set of principles emerged in Springdale that allowed student and professional agency to grow and flourish. If the Game Plan describes the moves you might make, think of these principles as the ground rules.

Chapter 6

The Game Plan for Professional Agency

> Our teachers want to be supportive of their students, but many felt uncomfortable with the "how" of addressing tough topics or how to say the "right things" to students. (Sugg 2019)

While we consistently, doggedly focused on *Putting Students First*, we never lost sight of the critical educator role. Springdale teachers, administrators, counselors, paraprofessionals, and others were expected to function in new ways. Springdale educators captured the vision of student-centered environments and began seeking ways to improve practices so that student voice and choice were raised.

Professional agency, the freedom to guide and explore their own learning, enabled this.

ESTABLISH A LEADERSHIP PLAN

- Logic Modeling
- Ongoing Design and Action Planning

In education, we use a lot of different jargon for similar concepts. You might think of a leadership plan as a *strategic plan*, or a *conceptual framework*, or a *theory of change*, or something else altogether. But what mattered, in our case, was having a clear, reliable description of what we wanted to do, and why. Given our emphasis on evidence-based practice, we needed to open up the black box and describe how all the parts fit together.

Our initial leadership plan was codified in a 2014 logic model (Springdale Public Schools 2014) (see figure 6.1). Our goals were to increase student

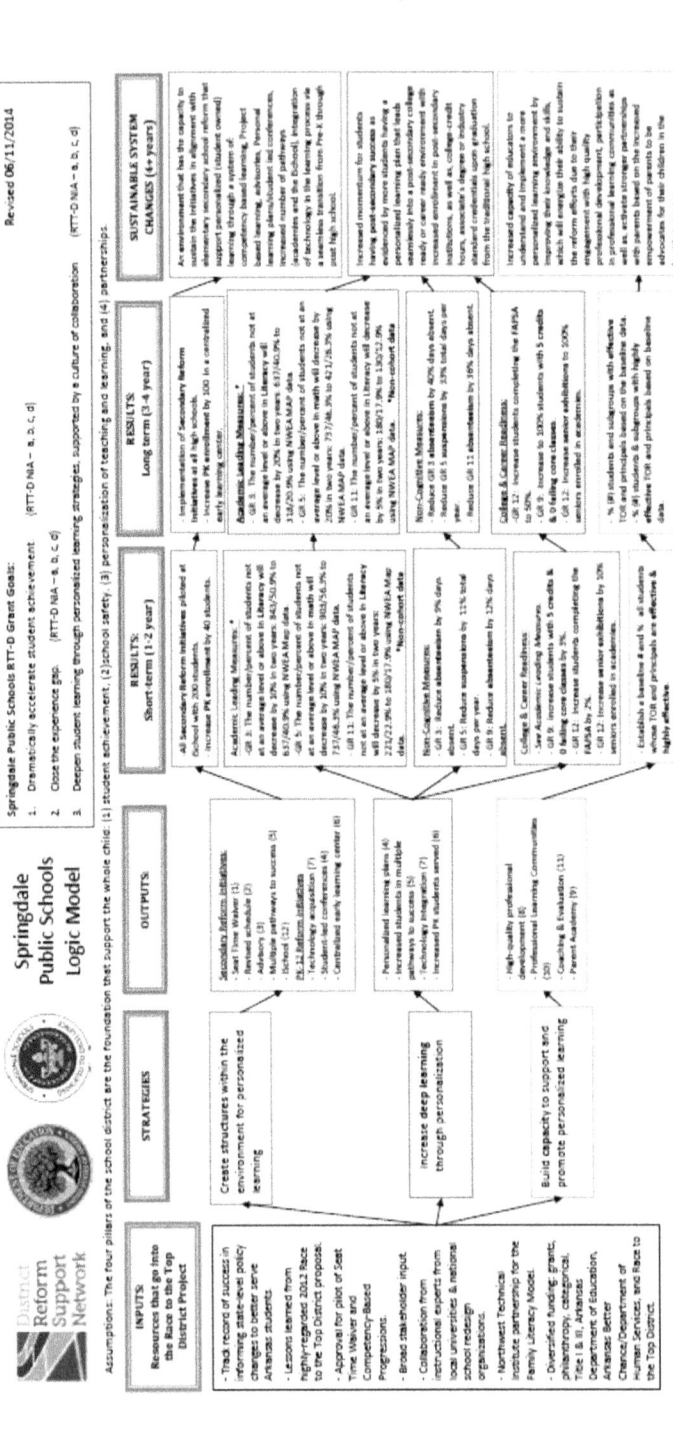

Figure 6.1 Springdale Public Schools Logic Model. Springdale Public Schools, 2014.

achievement, close achievement gaps, and personalize learning. The model describes three primary strategies and eleven project-level outputs. Gathering all this information and arranging it in ways that made sense was a difficult, time-consuming task but very worthwhile. Although this was admittedly a chore, in the end we found the logic model to be of tremendous value in keeping us all on the same page and focused on our vision.

The first order of business was designing the logic model, based on some loosely connected beliefs about improving student engagement. We had a collection of ideas based on research, gut feelings, and examples in practice. However, the actual work of designing a logic model to guide our work was new to our team.

Thanks to our Race to the Top District grant, we received technical support and guidance from the US Department of Education. The federal program officers introduced us to the art and science of creating useful logic models. During the design phase we shared the developing framework with the patron shelf, the school board, and the teacher leadership committee (Springdale's "Joint Council"). Based on lots of feedback the district-level leadership team moved forward, adjusting and developing implementation plans for each project.

There are many templates available for use in generating a logic model. What really matters is getting to the heart of what you want to accomplish, defined over a period of time. That means being explicit about your short-term goals, long-term goals, and sustainable outcomes. Once your goals and outcomes are set, determine the types of activities that will support your capacity to achieve them.

This process is not linear even though in the aforementioned narrative it may appear to be so. In reality, the plan changes and evolves with clarifying conversations, friendly debate, and "chicken or egg"—or in our case—project or strategy discussions.

The same thing was true about our sustainable outcomes—this section of the logic model really pushed us to think into the future and be specific about the residual and ongoing effects of our work. We set our measurable short-term (first and second year) and long-term (third to fifth year) goals but found defining our "Sustainable Outcomes" was one of the most challenging, but worthwhile, exercises. The conversation around sustainable outcomes required deeper thinking and looking more than five years into our future to visualize our ideal system.

Let me give you an example. One of our earliest initiatives focused on flexible scheduling. We know flexibility is needed to respond to a changing world, and we started by thinking about scheduling and time as short-term goals. But as we shifted our thinking to sustainable outcomes we quickly realized what we really wanted was an environment filled with practices that are flexible to innovation. Thus, our immediate project definitions may evolve over time—but the mind-set of keeping our school environments nimble in the face of change is important for long-term sustainability.

Of course, by definition, logic models are static. They generally describe what you plan to do, or perhaps what you are doing, and *predict* the outcomes and impact. We are still engaged in learning about the relationships between specific activities and their relationships to impacts like increased student achievement. A static, prospective logic model was a good starting point, but it lacked the information needed to promote and sustain school improvement.

Aligned with the logic model, we began to develop design and action plans for supporting activities that had more flexibility and allowed for tweaks and adjustments over the course of our work. In other words, the logic model was the overarching map for our journey toward taking personalization to the next level. The design and action plans detailed the operational minutiae that could be adjusted and tweaked based on the current conditions.

Support for this methodology is found within the Design and Action Plan (DAP) (Yamaguchi, et al. 2017, 47) approach to specify and codify key components of program design. The DAP helps us think more flexibly about what we are doing as we learn and modify our plan based on experience.

At the telling of this story, lots of initiatives are in place. For the sake of transparency, it is important to acknowledge that in every single case, initiatives were put into place in small steps or over several years. The Logic Model provided the foundation for setting specific targets for the twelve projects identified within grant period. Each of the twelve projects had a "rollout" schedule.

> Tick-tock . . . tick-tock . . . . We easily fall into the rhythms of time in our lives. We have rhythms for sleeping, eating working and playing. Schools are bound by rhythms, and they become fixed in our thinking as resolute and unchanging. Imagine if your systems of regulating, financing, teaching, and learning were not captive to time, but, instead were allowed to occur anytime, anyplace, anyhow, and at any pace, learning in a continuum of mastery. (Bramante and Colby 2012, 1–2)

As with any desired plans of action, there are also the realized plans of action. If we were ahead of schedule all was well and good. In the case of expanding the Pre-K model, we were able to accelerate our scheduled implementation rollout due to a grant the district received.

Of all the initiatives mentioned, the implementation and spread of technology was one of the most challenging. We were making huge investments in grades PK-12. However, in the case of the technology action plan, the original idea of expanding by grade level was changed completely. Initially, the plan called for a systematic rollout beginning in the elementary grades. Once the technology team reviewed the plan, they determined that this was not the best model going forward.

The plan was shifted so that schools with older technology received the upgrade in technology first regardless of grade level. They also knew that they could only handle a certain number of new computers at one time, given the wiring and configuration requirements. A schedule was created and posted so that everyone knew when it would be their turn.

Many related decisions had to be made about which devices for which grades, policies for students' use and penalties for misuse, tracking of breakage and repairs, tracking of missing equipment, and other accountability issues. We were solving issues such as whether or not to let students check devices out, keep them all day, take them home. We were concerned about the quality of use—was the new equipment simply a substitution for pencil, paper, and the overhead, or were students and faculty taking advantage of the technology for research, online communications, and deeper learning?

Questions were being asked by faculty members: Which websites were appropriate, which were not? Could teachers bring their own websites and apps into the system—what about viruses? Can we trust our students to stay off inappropriate sites? What happens when we start academic testing and the system freezes or bumps kids off? Getting the hardware out to schools had to be tempered with thoughtful procedures about how to maintain the integrity of the system with both the hardware and software.

Another example of plans shifting and evolving happened with our Career Academies. Our original plan for a single medical academy quickly bumped up against greater student interest than we anticipated. The plan called for one cohort of students to experience this pathway through high school. A partnership with a local hospital was established so students could gain workplace experience. Many meetings were held and assurances were given, on both sides. We thought it wise to have a memorandum of understanding at the outset, so everyone at school and at the hospital knew what was expected.

But soon after introducing the program we realized we did not have enough slots to meet the demands. In addition, we had students whose schedules did not allow them to participate in the full academy pathway. At first, during the first few years, we were rather strict—you were either in the academy or you were not. But after experiencing the disappointment of our students, we changed our stance.

We addressed this by expanding some of sections and allowing students to enroll in single courses. This enabled students who had an interest in medical sciences to take some of the courses without being in the academy. They did not get as many of the experiences as those in the academy—but at least they could take advantage of the content. Over time, we expanded the number of faculty as well as the number of cohorts as the demand for the program deemed it appropriate.

Due to the success of this model of personalizing the pathway through high school, the decision was made to add more academy options for students. In order to determine which academies to add, we surveyed the business community as well as the students. Over the next few years, we added the Information and Technology Academy, Architecture and Engineering Academy, a Teaching Academy, and a Law and Public Safety Academy.

The list can go on and on. I think we were overly ambitious to get all our initiative implemented in a very short period of time. We survived all of the start-up frustrations and issues—but in hindsight, we were very naïve about the complexity of what we were doing.

Creating and sustaining a DAP takes time, and as long as you are learning about your programs it will evolve and change. The process requires continually revisiting action plans and rebalancing competing interests and resources. Activities are assessed for challenges, resources, and to see how they can work together to leverage the strengths of each. But they are also assessed in terms of the potential impact. We often found the easiest to implement solutions, the so-called low hanging fruit, never offered much in terms of impact.

We always knew our goal of personalization was going to take effort and learning to reach, so we embraced the opportunity to tackle challenges. Looking at multiple, possible actions together through the DAP process helps us find high-payoff pathways.

The leadership planning process forces our team to look at both the big picture and the details. Over the years we discover timelines and actions were not accurate or well thought out, so we adjust them to reflect the reality of our implementation work. We take care to report on and share these changes and evolutions publicly. For example, status reports are shared with the school board on a monthly basis to keep them involved with, and appraised of, the work.

PROVIDE FLEXIBLE SCHEDULES

- Competency-based learning
- Online and blended learning

As with many of our initiatives, we began the work with conversations about the barriers the existing time-bound schedule erected, and how they stood in the way of what students really needed. We also invited one of the authors of "Off the Clock" (Bramante and Colby 2012) as part of a book study that broadened our thinking about ways to use time in school.

Although the title speaks to scheduling, the heart of this component is moving the basic structure of our schools toward a competency-based system. Flexible schedules ensure all students can successfully develop the knowledge and skills they need for success by focusing on mastering essential standards. Springdale schools are deliberately moving away from traditional, time- and place-bound structures, including the Carnegie Unit.

We appealed to our State Department of Education for waivers from certain seat time requirements based on the Carnegie Unit. We also discovered we could adjust our existing schedule to include school day advisories. It is hard to anticipate how various schools will be able to react to the time variable. But is it well worth the discussion and the conversation to see what flexibility may exist.

The Carnegie Unit is a time-bound and time-honored hallmark of traditional education, created to ensure sufficient time was afforded in the study of subject matter (the traditional Carnegie model is 120 hours of seat time over a full school year). In practice, the concern for clock time has overshadowed the expectation for the depth and quality of learning.

In this traditional model, students can "pass" a class and earn credit knowing only 60 percent of the material, even though they might benefit (and learn more!) given additional time. Some students might master *all* the material in considerably fewer hours, but their pace is not taken into consideration either. Time, not learning, is the variable that controls the traditional system.

Administrators enable flexible scheduling initiatives by shaping policies that allow innovative models to flourish. In Springdale's case, we required explicit permission from the Arkansas Department of Education to create different types of learning environments for students. We sought, and received, waivers for a number of state-required structural elements. Administrators are also responsible for engaging the community in a discussion of the benefits of competency-based learning. They need to provide the resources, including time, for teachers to learn about competency-based approaches and align curriculum, instruction, and assessment. Technology systems with the ability to track and report on student mastery were needed.

The role of the teacher is redefined to *facilitator of learning*. This is a major shift for many and requires a nurturing approach. Teachers must work together to create mastery-based systems, and need time to prioritize standards and explore assessments that reflect student voice and choice. They need support as they learn how to guide students toward mastery.

Student roles change as well, and it is worth remembering that we need to explicitly support this shift as well. In a flexible system, students take ownership of their learning and make choices to support success.

Policy waivers and changes allowed us to pilot programs that replaced "seat time" credit with standards-based mastery demonstrations. They also allowed us to insert an advisory period into the school day and have high school students participate in internships for credit. Today's options for accessing technology-enabled online learning represent a radical change to the traditional student schedule. Competency-based learning provides students across the district with opportunities to choose how and when they demonstrate proficiency. Personalized learning plans address advancement tied to mastery.

Changes continue in Springdale. The Don Tyson School of Innovation is moving closer to a full mastery learning model. As a result, students can be accelerated through their high school program of study and complete higher education courses as part of their school day. Students at Don Tyson also have the ability to mix online learning with on-campus experiences. All secondary schools have adjusted their schedules to allow for advisory periods combined with targeted times for students to receive remediation or enrichment opportunities.

Traditional thinking was that all remediation time should be after school. For many of our students this was not possible due to transportation issues, family circumstances, and financial situations. The change in mind-set that remediation could and should occur during the school day came about as more flexibility in the use of school time was considered by each school.

At the elementary level, we are shifting the way we think about grading. Elementary school report cards now reflect both achievement and growth measures. One absolute grade is not sufficient to indicate the complexity of the learning process. Families are now given richer, more detailed information about the accomplishments of their students.

Technology has also expanded time for learning. Legislation was recently passed in Arkansas that allows students and teachers to convene via technology on "weather days"—days when the conditions for getting to school are difficult or dangerous. This option is called "Alternate Method of Instruction," and is preapproved by the Arkansas Department of Education each year prior to use. Secondary students can take their computers home so their learning time is extended, or as importantly, not limited by lack of access to technology. Elementary students have a virtual or physical option for instruction based on individual student needs.

Unsurprisingly, flexible scheduling is complicated, and time constraints do not completely disappear. But the solutions arising are rich and varied and they extend learning in many ways. Every time we provide more flexible learning we give students more options and help them tailor experiences that truly fit their needs.

REFLECT AND USE FEEDBACK TO IMPROVE

- Professional Learning Communities
- Hard and Soft Data

Professional learning communities require preparation on the part of the leadership and the faculty to ensure fidelity to the model. We found it best to provide authentic professional development from leading consultants who have the tools and resources needed to establish a strong foundation.

Initially, a few teachers attended outside workshops on professional learning communities. We quickly discovered that we could provide on-site summer institutes for a much larger number of faculty members if we brought the experts to us instead of sending a small number of folks out of town. All schools were able to have participants during the summer institutes to discover firsthand the value and structure of authentic professional learning communities (PLCs). We were able to underwrite some of the expense by inviting other districts to send teams. Our local educational cooperative was also providing institutes during the school year for schools in the region. We took advantage of all opportunities to have faculty trained.

When planning for the institutes, we found it most effective to have teacher teams that included at least one administrator. The roles and responsibilities of all were presented and discussed so that the requirements were clear to all concerned. Since a large network of schools were involved, solutions to issues were often the topic of district meetings like principal roundtable discussions. Barriers that were coming up were shared and solutions were considered.

We discovered it was critically important to distinguish PLCs from a standard grade-level or department meeting. In a PLC process you are concerned with improving and or extending student achievement through targeted instructional processes based on formative assessment. Although many other important activities occur during teacher planning time (calling families, grading papers, and lesson planning, for example), once teams enter into a PLC process the focus is only on how individual students are achieving and how instructional practices and curricular design support their learning.

Key to making PLCs work is the leadership provided by building-level principals and lead teachers. They ensure the schedule supports time for teams to meet, and that appropriate agendas and norms are established. An outcome of the PLC process is a strong personalized professional development model. As improvements in professional practice emerge from the discussion about what did and did not connect with students and their learning, faculty members provide job-embedded support for one another by reflecting on, and sharing, successful practices.

Strong PLCs rely on an effective system of data collection and data sharing. It can be as simple as looking at student work samples together, or rely on a more sophisticated system of formative assessments. It is the discussion of evidence related to the achievement of each child that is so central to success. This cannot be accomplished without some type of data. Both hard and soft data are appropriate for discussion.

The problem-solving tool known as root cause analysis helped us uncover important insights and solutions. Rather than jumping to conclusions about poor performance data, assigning fault to lack of student effort or poor instruction, this analysis surfaces more meaningful, and actionable, results.

For example, one school found the cause of poor performance on standardized tests in geometry at the fourth grade was a misalignment between the curriculum and pacing guide. The pacing guide did not include enough time for the foundation work in geometry in grades K-3 so fourth-grade students had not worked with some of the basic geometry skills. A vertical team conversation looking at the curriculum maps pinpointed the problem very quickly based on the problematic student data.

At George Elementary School in Springdale, informal evidence and feedback arises at:

- Weekly leadership team meetings, including student representation;
- Weekly grade-level professional learning community meetings;
- Bimonthly faculty professional development sessions; and
- Teacher selected learning inquiry projects.

(Freeman 2019)

Soft data is very useful when looking at the unique issues related to individual children. In a recent discussion, teachers found that certain students were inattentive and lethargic at the start of the day. Are we seeing lazy or difficult students? Or was there something else at play? A deeper dive into the soft data noted that these particular students were eligible for the school breakfast program but were not taking advantage of it.

A review of the timing of breakfast and the arrival of the buses through the root cause analysis quickly determined that something different had to happen with the breakfast schedule or the arrival of the buses if we wanted these children to have time to eat. In this case extending the breakfast period was the best solution. Students came to class ready to work after a nutritious breakfast. Seems so logical and simple—but it took deliberate conversations focused on the data (time allowed for breakfast, arrival schedule of the buses) to provide an authentic solution.

Professional learning communities are everywhere in Springdale. They exist at the district and school level, as well as at grade levels. Every educator in the Springdale School District actively participates in at least one professional learning community, based on the process described by Rick DuFour (1998). This professional learning structure incorporates ongoing feedback and improvement cycles at all levels.

Vertical content teams are working on curriculum and articulation, and cross-school teams are addressing common problems of practice. All professional learning communities in Springdale are committed to achieving better outcomes for students. The focus is always on results, with progress measured through formative assessment. In keeping with the spirit of personalization in Springdale, the mechanisms used by individual teams vary, but all use protocols to discuss data and members are always mutually accountable.

Our experience with the Race to the Top grant accelerated our sophistication with the use of data. Those who are familiar with federal grants know that there are lots and lots of data points to be collected and analyzed. It quickly became apparent that we did not have a consistent or standardized plan for data collection.

Full disclosure of the data is important for public confidence and accountability of our work. Each year the data were collected, reported, and posted publicly. Determining appropriate interpretation of data meant a dispassionate review without bias. We can't always blame the scale when we don't like the data we are getting. Courageous conversations occurred each time the data team met. Are the data accurate? How do we know? What are the data telling us? What can we do better next time?

Upgrading to a uniform collection of data requires establishing precise formats, timelines, and definitions. For example, enrollment data and graduation rates are examples of shifts in our growing competence in the use of data. Answering the question, "How many students do you have in the district?" seems straightforward until you realize a growing district will disclose different numbers on any given day. Looking at enrollment figures at only point per year can also mask important demographic patterns. For example, families may move in and out of Springdale if they are engaged in seasonal or migratory work. We defined, and began using, a number of explicit measures of enrollment, including things like "day one" and maximum enrollment over an eight-week period.

Graduation rate is another statistic that is often used or interpreted out of context. Generally, we use the "four-year cohort" graduation rate for reporting purposes and comparison with traditional schools across the nation. This measure essentially conveys the percentage of a ninth-grade cohort that graduates in four years following a traditional path. But we were engaged in creating nontraditional pathways and programs for students, and we saw equal value in students who graduated within three years, or five years. If we were going to use graduation rate as a measure of success, we needed to carefully define what we were measuring.

A final example of the value of good, explicit data related to our efforts to decrease chronic absenteeism. We had set a district attendance goal of 95 percent but really didn't understand how to think about the other 5 percent of students. Meaningful conversations and solutions came when the faculty began looking at students who were in that category. Who were those students who were missing twenty, thirty, or forty days of school? Once the principals, counselors, and teachers became more aware of the specific children who fell into this category, targeted work began to address their barriers to coming to school.

Proactive work on the part of caring adults in each school had a profound effect. Chronic absenteeism dropped over the course of four years from 20 percent in grade three to 9 percent. Grades five and nine demonstrated equally impressive results: grade five changed from 19 percent to 8 percent and in grade nine, the numbers fell from 26 percent to 12 percent (Avery and Cervone 2017).

Getting to this broad level of success required a lasting commitment from administrators to make time, training, data, and support available. While the district does not micromanage the teams, they do hold teams accountable for meeting the mission of the PLC process. That may mean building leaders attending meetings as resource or facilitator, or suggesting design adjustments. Ensuring team members have timely access to student assessment data is another key role played by administrators.

Teachers and other team members need the skills to participate and a commitment to the team and process. In practice that means knowing how to gather and interpret data, the ability to reflect on instructional practice, and a willingness to collaborate and learn from others.

The takeaway from this is that as leaders we are not afraid of what the data tells us. It is always nice to hear all is well, but real learning arises when the data point out a need for improvement. Importantly, we do not shy away from our innovations in the face of difficulties. We brainstorm and explore modifications, or entirely new ways of reaching our goal.

CONNECT WITH COMMUNITY

- Family Literacy
- Family Involvement
- Student-Led Conferences
- Career Academies

Schools should reflect their community needs and wants. Therefore, first steps in this area suggest community conversations. Examples of good community conversation questions include: What does the community value in its schools? What does the community need from its graduates? How can we increase the participation of families and patrons in the schools? How can we increase the connections between our community and our students?

Family/community surveys have served our school district well. When we first instituted student-led conferences we provided exit surveys so that families could tell us what worked and what needed improvement. We made important changes to the model based on this feedback. We were also able to use the overwhelming support shown on survey to assure ourselves that the new practice was benefiting students and families alike.

Building confidence and a comfort zone with families who do not speak English required the use of translators and translated materials. At first this may seem awkward and expensive; however, it is a basic requirement for an inclusive environment. With our newest community members, the Marshallese community, we found small focus groups with translators more useful than printed surveys. These discussions helped us establish stronger connections between the schools, families, and community. This was done both at the district level with the superintendent as well as at building levels where Marshallese children attended.

Community outreach is a two-way street and it is energizing to seek collaborative partners and volunteers from your community. School faculty members volunteer in the summer to provide book vans for neighborhood children who want access to books but cannot get to the library. Community churches, businesses, and groups like Kiwanis Club, Rotary Club, and the Springdale Police Department provide special gifts at holidays and coordinate community clothing and food drives. Volunteers work throughout the year as mentors and tutors for Springdale students.

Curricular experiences are enhanced through business and sister school real-world partnerships. Community-based experts in the field of science and technology help students explore the relevance and application of math, science, and technology. Students act as valued assets to local businesses by interning as information technology specialists, web designers, and nursing assistants. Truly, the sky is the limit when working with your local chamber of commerce members, faith-based organizations, and civic clubs to extend learning for all children. All you need to do is start the conversation.

> At a "patron shelf" meeting, students shared their experiences with technology-supported projects. Community members reacted positively to what the students had to share. This clearly helped to get community member acceptance of the change. Putting students up front appeared to be both the norm and a positive way to convey needed changes. (DiMartino 2019)

Schools reflect community. Historically, the Springdale community has set high expectations for close working relationships with the local chamber of commerce, civic groups, and family/booster groups. The wider community is invited to provide input to the work of the district through the *Patron Shelf*— a place where a broad spectrum of folks come to collaborate, suggest solutions, and discuss educational issues. This long-standing working partnership provides a confident, broad-based foundation that supports innovative solutions targeted toward improving education for all.

Establishing strong, working communication channels with the community is critical to the success of any school system. The superintendent, Dr. Rollins, played a significant role in communicating with the community via the school board and the chamber of commerce. Monthly school board reports delivered verbally and in writing are provided on major initiatives.

School board meetings are scheduled at school sites, during the day, promoting relationships and letting students, teachers, and staff speak directly to policy makers and the community at large. Principals created excellent presentations showcasing the shifts in practice. Students were invited to share their stories about what they were experiencing with increased agency in their school curriculum and student-led conferences.

School board work sessions have sections devoted to the work of the change initiatives. Site visits to all schools by community and state leaders give a sense of what the work is all about. Expressed concerns and questions are taken seriously. What were the root causes of the concerns, what could be changed to correct it—or what misinformation was needed to be corrected? With any major innovation, there are some bound to be minor missteps and corrections needed along the way. Critical to the processes were the ongoing communication loops that kept us all talking to one another.

As a community, we took explicit steps to ensure all voices in the community were represented. An "open invitation" is not sufficient, rather conscious effort and deliberate planning are needed to ensure connections are built (and honored) with families who have been historically underrepresented. Families who had been reluctant or hesitant to engage with the schools must be individually identified, and personal communications established.

Roughly half of our students are emergent bilinguals, and most of their family members are immigrants learning English. We built a unique, research-based program designed to engage the family members through English language development and literacy instruction, while nurturing the relationship between school and home. The Springdale Family Literacy Program has family members come to their child's school for twelve hours per week. That time is split between adult English as a second language instruction, time volunteering their child's classroom, and time learning about the Springdale school system and community. Free daycare is provided to remove barriers for families with young children.

The family literacy program has a complementary family leadership development program (PTLA—Parents Taking Leadership Action). The PTLA meets several times a week as part of the Family Literacy program, to help parents understand they are part of the process of teaching and learning. They focus on modeling ways for families to find and use their own voices and become advocates for their children. The work of the PTLA extends beyond the school, and introduces immigrant families to the structures and organizations of Springdale, including law enforcement, local businesses, and municipal government. PTLA participants complete a legacy project, often a brief information segment for broadcast on the local Spanish language radio program.

Springdale also provides other avenues for family investment in their child's education. We aim to create seamless partnerships between schools and families. Parents participate on school improvement and planning committees, on parent-teacher organizations, and on a variety of booster groups. All communication, written and oral, needs to be available in the home languages of the community and administrators are responsible for finding the mechanisms and resources needed to make this work.

At the local level, principals and teachers need to embrace the value of family involvement, and ask questions about what works in every situation. Principals and teachers need to focus on the needs of the families and provide resources and knowledge that can help foster partnerships for student success. At the classroom level, teachers need to convey enthusiasm for working with families, and make sure they are providing an inviting classroom. Springdale teachers routinely communicate "grows and glows" to families, sharing positive news and observations about their child.

Students play an important role in community connections as well, and need to understand why it is important for their families and community members to be involved. Student-led conferences, career academies, and internships are all vehicles that require students to interface with family members and other adults in the community. Students have an obligation to be honest, positive representatives of themselves and their schools when working with their own families and community representatives.

Chapter 7

The Game Plan for Student Agency

When I can share what I am doing, it is a lot better. It's not just the teacher's opinion. We are trying harder to meet our goals since we know we will have to share them with our parents. (Student 2018, Helen Tyson Middle and JB Hunt Elementary Schools)

The Game Plan includes explicit expectations for students. Highlighting the roles and responsibilities of students authentically reflects our belief that this work is best done in partnership with students. Although there are many ways to define and organize the Game Plan components, taken together these elements should lead to an increase in student agency. Examples of shifts in practice included things like student advisory councils, listening to student input regarding the daily operations of the school, structured opportunities for goal setting through advisories, giving voice and choice within the context of new curriculum designs, and opportunities for students to engage in meaningful dialogue about their hopes, dreams, and desires with teachers and families.

PROVIDE VOICE AND CHOICE FOR STUDENTS

- Personal Learning Plans
- Student-Led Conferences

There are several simple ways to begin supporting student voice and choice. We began with allowing more flexibility within the lesson plan design so that students could choose from a list of books to read or provide alternatives in how they demonstrated their learning in the assessment models. In the early stages you can include student leadership teams to advise the principal on assemblies of interest, playground issues, food choices in the cafeteria, or end-of-year celebrations.

Students can be wonderful ambassadors to newcomers and guests in the building. In almost every facet, with a little creativity, there are opportunities for students to be connected and involved with the daily life of the school.

To move to the next level, teachers and students can work together and create rubrics to assess learning. This is especially useful if the community is already engaged in project-based learning and using rubrics to define success and assess impact. Students and teachers can engage in conversations about what excellence looks like and present their findings on a poster or PowerPoint; for example, teachers can provide exemplars from which even the youngest students can draw conclusions.

Technology provides a variety of tools that promote voice and choice. When a teacher provides the activities of the day via Google Classroom, for example, students may be able to choose to complete their math practice, their writing activity, or their social studies research in any order throughout the day.

> Excellence will be achieved when we have more engaged students who are learning by building knowledge, making meaning, and applying understanding on their own and they can verbalize the process as it makes sense to them. (Freeman 2019)

As students enter high school and have more options for online learning they can access additional coursework and accelerate their progress, or secure more time if needed. This is the model that is at the heart of the Don Tyson School of Innovation. Students have considerable control of their time, and can even complete an associate degree program of study while completing their high school career.

Students can also have a voice in setting the behavior expectations for the classroom. Classroom rules established by students set a far different tone than a teacher-driven set of rules with punitive consequences. Schools can effectively use class meetings to discuss the consequences of poor behavior choices and set about resolving the issues. A simple example is giving students a voice and choice in actions such as who they sit with, where they sit, and what type of chair they sit on while maintaining proper attention to their independent work.

Advancing student voice and choice requires the adults in the system to relinquish total control and provide options for students to contribute. This may be the hardest part since we are accustomed to being in control. Students may need encouragement to share their interests and concerns, since they, too, may not have been invited to be part of the school conversation in the past. This isn't just about a shift in academic practice.

In reality, we are creating a process of ownership by students and preparing them for what lies ahead as they mature and become more and more responsible in life. Starting the shift to student-owned climate for learning in their primary years will provide great benefits as students enter secondary school less reliant on others to tell them what to do.

In many ways, increasing student voice and choice is at the heart of all of our work. The overarching intent is to create opportunities for students to be partners in the learning process. The focus of our personalization process is to give students the capacity to become self-directed, ask for help when needed, and make connections to the relevance of what they are learning. Students should not fear failure, but know that mistakes are part of the learning process and are part of the problem-solving equation. All of these attributes (and more) are what we hope the shifts in practice reveal in students.

Providing voice and choice for students is an essential component for establishing a personalized learning environment. The word that is most operational here is *provide*. The adults in charge must relinquish unilateral control in order to *provide* opportunities for voice and choice. Today we see the impact of increased student voice in things like our curriculum and assessments, and in ways technology is used to support learning. Student engagement on advisory councils broadly impacts the activities and policies of each school.

Across the district students can express choice in learning through programs like the *Education Accelerated by Service and Technology* (EAST) program. EAST provides access to unique technologies, allowing students opportunities to identify and address a plethora of projects. All activities within these programs are student driven, and students at all levels have developed amazing projects. Projects are diverse and meaningful.

One heartfelt example includes the creation of an adaptive device to fit on a bicycle so a child with a missing hand can ride her bike. Many were brought to tears when the young lady rode her bike for the first time. A significant project from Springdale High School involved students capturing and recording stories from the Second World War veterans through the Greatest Generation project. These stories are now housed in Washington DC thanks to a partnership with the Shiloh Museum in Springdale.

Voices of our learners are included in various ways across the district. George Elementary School involves students during monthly "Growing Giant" Celebration Assemblies, where students plan and carry out the events of the day. Westwood Elementary has their fifth-grade students plan events on the last day of school, with teacher guidance. Everyone has a responsibility on that day, and then gets to enjoy fun-planned activities. In many Springdale schools students serve as "lunch ambassadors" and meet with cafeteria staff to help plan menus. Students also serve as liaisons and special friends to students newly arriving in school. Students can share concerns and offer solutions to problems they perceive are occurring in most classrooms during daily class meetings.

Tyson Elementary school instituted *Passion Projects*, where students choose a problem to explore and then share what they did and learned with their peers. For example, a group of students developed free lending libraries for the community as a way of providing better access to books for students and their families. Tyson Elementary also offers *extra learning opportunities* (ELOs) to extend learning.

Students at Tyson Elementary can access the ELO for additional help by signing up with teachers for a mini-lesson in an area where they need to strengthen their skills. The ELO may be provided via technology, or by a peer who has mastered the skill. Students can also take advantage of ELOs for enrichment or exploration, with teachers who offer special classes in areas of personal interest or expertise in topics such as chess. This builds relationships as well as new skills.

Elementary teachers are providing students opportunities for choice in the organization of the classroom. Students are offered the responsibility for things like taking attendance, lunch counts, handing out and collecting papers. One innovative group of students at Shaw Elementary wanted to have a special job for a member of the class—the official joke teller. This student helped start the day with a funny (preapproved) joke or story!

Students have choices in their places to do independent work—on a rug, on a ball/chair at their desk, or on a bean bag chair at Smith, Harp and Jones Elementary, to name just three. All of these choices come with accountability and responsibility to follow classroom rules and finish tasks on time.

When more freedom is given, more responsibility is required. Some schools instituted the concept of *Trust Badges*, given to students who demonstrate excellence as a citizen of their school. These badges allow students to go to the library or work in the maker space, or have more independence within the activities of the school.

Every student in Springdale is engaged in the development and use of a personal learning plan, designed to responsibly identify and progress toward short- and long-term goals. This planning process helps students assess their status on the learning continuum, and adds relevance to their coursework as they develop career goals. Students author the plan, with guidance and input from advisors, teachers, family, and community members. In Springdale we support the development and revisiting of personal learning plans through advisory.

The personal learning plan forms the basis for student-led conferences. These conferences create opportunities for students to showcase their own learning for their families, and directly invest families in their child's education and goal setting. The conference is an opportunity for students and parents to decide about the future while equipping students with the skills needed to explain their learning and thinking.

Administrators need to provide time and professional development for staff, students, and families if they are expected to develop a system where every student has a personal learning plan and engages in student-led conferencing. Teachers and/or advisors need to work effectively within an advisory period to develop and maintain these plans, and prepare students for the student-led conference. Data on student progress needs to be readily available and understandable.

Students are responsible for effectively and responsibly using their voices and choices to advance their own learning. They need to engage thoughtfully in the personal learning plan process and set good, realistic goals for themselves. They need to understand their own progress and reflect honestly on that progress in conversations with their teachers and families. Students and parents often need direct guidance and support before they can engage in meaningful, reflective conversations.

HAVE STUDENTS READY TO LEARN

- Pre-K Program

This section of the game plan can have broad application at all levels of school. Ideally, all students will benefit from school if all students arrive ready to learn. Our particular focus was on expanding Pre-K education to impact high needs students. We believed that getting young children ready for school would benefit our families, our teachers, and our community. Springdale's Pre-K classrooms encourage exploration, self-expression, curiosity, language development, and positive social interaction.

In Springdale, our first hurdle was shifting the community perception of our charge as a school district, from K-12 to Pre-K-12. In our case, the need to get a large number of emergent bilingual Pre-K children into an environment where they could receive English instruction and practice was an urgent driver. Realistically, students in our community need to be fluent in English and we knew this preparation was essential for success in kindergarten.

The exposure to the pre-literacy and pre-numeracy skills paid off well. So, a word to the wise, what happens before students come to school in kindergarten matters a lot. We chose to take those children under our watch in order to strengthen the system from top to bottom.

Once our mind-set about the need for Pre-K had changed, we became students of Pre-K education. The rules and regulations for Pre-K children are a world unto themselves so we had a lot of learning to do. We sought grants to help pay for the staff and the materials required, worked with the regulatory agencies, and opened our enrollment process for the first year with fingers crossed.

> The Pre-K curriculum intentionally builds relationship skills. Springdale Pre-K graduates are expected to be able to independently use their learning to make choices that affect their relationship with the environment and distinguish between helpful and hurtful choices.

The response was overwhelming. If you are considering this, be prepared for an overwhelming interest. We served 100 percent of our capacity and had a waiting list that first year that would have doubled our enrollment.

Pre-K students are encouraged to establish a sense of agency through a day filled with voice and choice. Students have centers or areas of interest to stimulate literacy and numeracy skills, as well as areas for exploring science, homemaking, the arts, and building. Outdoors, students choose to ride trikes, climb, swing, play outdoor musical instruments, do outdoor art, or just run and jump! Teachers encourage the three- and four-year-olds to experience all areas by inviting them to participate in all the activities. But, ultimately, students choose.

A foundational outcome of the early childhood program is self-directed behavior, and the curricular units feature these skills. We have found that even our youngest children can develop self-confidence and the skills to do research and share their research. For example, Pre-K students research a favorite animal and then create a presentation on an iPad to share with one another and guests. This is a favorite activity, and students are always comfortable and confident sharing what they learned.

Administrators need to ensure early childhood teachers are well trained and are preparing students for a successful transition to kindergarten. They also need to ensure the community understands the very specific and long-lasting benefits of these programs. We believe a high-quality early childhood education prepares and equips students for a successful future in school and in life. In addition to engaging learning environments, the Springdale program develops individual transition plans for kindergarten for students and their families. Wellness and health needs are also supported.

CREATE MULTIPLE PATHWAYS FOR STUDENTS

- Curriculum Design That Includes Choice
- Career Academies
- Alternative Learning Environments
- School of Innovation
- Anytime, Anyplace Learning via Technology

It begins with the belief system that one size does not fit all, a relatively new concept in the world of education. The factory model of schooling has been in effect for decades. You start on time, you end on time, and if you don't fit, you don't stay.

But, of course, our entire culture has changed. It used to be banking hours were from 9 to 3 and the only way to do your banking was to go to the marble halls of the bank itself. Now we can bank anywhere, anytime, anyplace. The same is true about education; learning happens outside the hours of 9–3 and you don't need to be in the school building itself. Exploring multiple pathways of learning is a way of tuning to the customized world we live in. Technology provides the flexibility we need.

We considered three issues as we looked at methods of providing multiple pathways. The first issue was to increase the engagement and connectedness of our high school students. We wanted to stem the dropout numbers by creating more relevant, career-based choices for students. Thus, the academies were born.

The second was the issue of students who were not succeeding in traditional school due to attendance and discipline issues. We visited schools where alternative education was thriving and brought back what would work here. We experimented with a night school approach, eventually replacing it with a day time alternative model.

The third issue was the huge transition to technology-based instruction. We began with a concentrated effort to move to a one-to-one technology model and offer online classes so that students could have more flexibility in accessing their courses. We saw our competitors in the private sector attracting our students with their increased flexibility, and accepted it as a challenge to provide that same level of flexibility within the public-school setting.

School leaders are advised to look at what issues are present in their community to determine what alternatives may be of value.

Individualization and differentiation of program options is a powerful method of personalizing education and building in student choice. We approached the idea of multiple pathways through overall curriculum design as well as through the creation of specific clustered program options.

The district selected the *Understanding by Design* framework (Wiggins and McTighe 2005) to help organize the standards into meaningful work for students. Courses of study are organized into units with specific attention to the required standards and supporting standards, along with assessments for and of learning. All teachers have online access to the full curriculum, along with a variety of materials to support learning, including resources and applied learning activities. Teachers are expected to tailor their lesson plans to fit the needs of their students and draw heavily from the provided materials. At the same time, teachers develop and contribute resources, ensuring our curriculum continues to evolve.

Figure 7.1 is an example of an applied learning activity drawn from our curriculum (Springdale Public Schools 2016). Springdale is the home of the *Naturals*, a minor league farm team for the Kansas City Royals. Each spring students are invited to attend a game at Arvest Ballpark. Of course, it is important to have a learning connection, so the district designed units of study specifically tied to the ballpark experience. This example shows how students may choose multiple pathways to learn and demonstrate their skills and knowledge.

Student Choice Board		
Research a famous baseball player from Arkansas Major League Players from Arkansas	Reaction Time: The Science of a Baseball Swing [3-minute Video]	How does the average number of runs (RBI) change from before the game to after the game for ten players? Graph to see a visual representation. Player Statistics before the Game NWA Naturals
Find out the Connection between Hot Springs, AR and baseball Hot Springs, AR Info	BASEBALL CHOICE BOARD	Create a baseball card about a classmate. Ask questions to answer the questions. Baseball Card
Read an article about economics (money)in baseball The Business of Baseball	Learn How a Major League Baseball is made! How It's Made: Baseball Video (5 minutes)	The Physics of Baseball: Forces and Motion [3-minute video]

Figure 7.1 Learning Activity Embedded in District Curriculum. Springdale Public Schools, 2016.

Springdale's full curriculum and related resources are freely available online, at https://sites.google.com/sdale.org/curriculum.

Secondary schools engage students in Career Academies. Students in the Springdale High School Medical Academy spend time at the hospital serving as volunteers. Springdale High students in the Law Academy serve as hosts when guests are arriving at special events at the school or other community venues, while supporting local law enforcement as extra sets of eyes and ears. The Architecture and Engineering Academy at Springdale High School assists in community development planning.

These examples build the student's sense of ownership to their pathway as well as contribute to the community. The Career Academy Model allows students to find relevance in their course work through specific connections to a broad array of careers. The structure of the academies is not intended to narrow the path to a specific field, rather it is to provide a broad understanding what the chosen pathway of study might offer.

An example of this is the Medical Academy. Students are exposed to a wide variety of career pathways found within the medical field of study. Becoming a doctor or a certified nursing assistant (CNA) or registered nurse (RN) are obvious pathways. However, students are also exposed to the other important roles in medicine such as lab techs, dietitians, medical researchers, pharmacists, and specialized fields such as pediatrics, gynecology, and geriatrics.

Springdale Career Academies are aligned with the National Standards of Practice for Career Academies. They are two- to four-year pathways that provide college preparatory curricula and engage students in postsecondary planning. Career academy students interface directly with the community through partnerships with employers, higher education institutions, and community organizations.

Another way of thinking about making pathways through high school more relevant is the "smaller communities of learning" model. Har-Ber High School has organized their students in grades ten to twelve into houses. These smaller groupings of students focus on a broad field of interest such as the sciences or the arts. Within those houses specific, smaller academies or communities can be found. This allows our large high schools to become "smaller" places, and ensures students can connect directly with teachers, counselors, and administrators.

Administrators play critical roles in ensuring Career Academies and other alternative pathways provide rigorous and equitable learning experiences that prepare students for postsecondary experiences. Administrators also need to ensure students are making thoughtful, well-informed choices that advance their personal goals. Like other initiatives, they need to make time, resources, and professional development available to support the full deployment of the programs.

Another pathway is through the Archer Learning Center, an alternative learning environment. This is a stand-alone high school for students needing a smaller community with more explicit social and academic support. Students who benefit from this program have challenges in their lives that make traditional school difficult. Attendance and discipline concerns are addressed head-on in a supporting environment that gives students a second chance at success.

Superintendent Dr. Rollins called out the importance of this pathway for Archer graduates, telling them, "Graduates you have done an excellent job. You have stayed the course. You did not give up when you could have. You could have quit and you did not. The lesson of perseverance that you have learned on your path will serve you well in life. You have shown the world you have what it takes" (J. Rollins, Speech to Archer HS Graduating Class 2019).

A major undertaking for the district was the establishment of a *school of innovation*, serving students in grades six through twelve. Students enrolled in the Don Tyson School of Innovation are choosing an alternative to the traditional secondary school, and have the opportunity to develop their own unique pathway through it.

The Don Tyson School of Innovation is named for, and honors, an innovator in the food industry, Don Tyson, founder of Tyson Foods. Tyson Foods is a company known for innovations in the poultry industry, a major industrial sector in Springdale. Naming this innovative school in honor of the Tyson family speaks to the strong legacy within this community of supporting innovation and change.

The Don Tyson School of Innovation is a place where we pilot new strategies to promote an ever more personalized learning environment. The fundamental tenets of the school are as follows:

- Students have the opportunity to accelerate their academic progressions with a waiver from the Carnegie Unit as a measure of course completion.
- Students have access to the curriculum supported by anytime, anyplace learning with flexibility in time and place. This includes an option for online course work for some or all classes.
- Students have an integrated approach to their studies with blocks of time to learn independently, in small groups, targeted instructional groups, or through applied learning experiences.
- Students have a technology-rich learning environment and smart classrooms and can take home computers.
- Students participate in real-world activities through project-based and problem-based activities.
- Students have an opportunity to attain career-specific credentials and/or an associate degree in cooperation with the regional community college.

Springdale took advantage of the need for a third high school to meet the growing student population, designing the physical structure to accommodate the Don Tyson School of Innovation from the ground up. Springdale Superintendent Dr. Rollins noted, "This building was designed to accelerate personalized learning. What we learn from this experience will impact how we renovate and design buildings in the future" (2019). This unique opportunity and the building in which it is housed is proving to be of great interest to educators from across the state and the nation.

SET GOALS WITH STUDENTS

- Advisory Programs
- Personal Learning Plans
- Student-Led Conferences

This is an area where we found the wisdom and guidance of others particularly helpful. We utilized the resources and support from the CSSR to set the stage for work in Springdale.

Goal setting needs to be done with useful evidence and data in hand. To make the work meaningful the data must be meaningful. We found formative reading data, rubrics used in the writing class, reading books moving from one reading level to another, or an increase in the number of books read were good examples of activities that helped set concrete goals that are meaningful to students. We also found classroom-wide or even grade-wide goals being set. For example, can 100 percent of students master their multiplication tables? Or, can 20 percent more students pass their spelling test on the first try?

Progress toward these lofty goals can be tracked and celebrated. These simple goal statements can bring synergy to a classroom of students who want to celebrate when meeting their goals.

Goal setting is not hard if you are not afraid of the data. Numbers simply give information. Getting over the fear of numbers is important for both teacher and student agency. Once we get past our fear of data, we can use the data to set goals that are reasonable and meaningful for all. There should be no sense of retribution in an ideal use of data. Rather, the environment needs to be one of a feeling of continuous improvement—and the data helps us along the way.

District leaders understand that many students are poorly motivated to learn by the traditional rewards and sanctions that middle and high schools have employed for a century. These "traditional" rewards and sanctions are not providing the lasting results we seek and desire as a community. We understand that students are motivated by the knowledge that there is an educator in the school building that cares about them. Connecting with students can be accomplished through regular meetings between small groups of students and educators within a school.

> Students need to be supported and guided in their journey. They need to be given their data about their achievement; templates that help them set goals; time during an advisory period to monitor their own progress toward those goals and be mentored about what lies ahead; and then share their strengths and areas of growth with a parent or other significant adult.
>
> In Springdale we began at the elementary level where principals and teachers accepted the challenge of a new definition of spring conferences where students did most of the talking. The process moved through the system throughout the next three years with fine-tuning and tweaking along the way. The process of engaging students in more meaningful ways does not look the same from the primary to the secondary, but the value of engagement is well understood. Essentially, we needed to find ways to empower the students in their own learning—doing school with students, not to students. While it seemed this would take more time to train the students to prepare to "report" to their parents, instead it became of way of our daily work. Student-led conferences were not a week of preparation; instead, it became the daily practice of having the students own their learning (Stewman 2019).

When we first started the conversation about personalization, we realized that the adults at school knew a lot about their students' progress and areas of growth. But the process was transformed when we made students part of the equation. This led us to the institution of student-led conferences, a foundational process in Springdale. We found the best way to engage students in the goal-setting process was to provide time during the day for advisory.

A key feature of advisory is helping students set goals for improvement, monitor their waypoints along the way, and provide support as needed to improve. Students have demonstrated a great capacity to embrace this concept. Principals in elementary and middle school report that students are very willing and able to set their goals and monitor their progress. By beginning this process in the early grades, the expectation that this is a part of the high school culture has gained momentum as the students move through school.

The advisory program at Har-Ber High School is an example of the impact the advisory process can have. Counselors and teachers at Har-Ber found students were bringing extremely personal concerns and complicated family matters to the attention of trusted advisors. Initially this made some teachers uncomfortable, and they worried about being unprepared to respond. But the advisory team addressed this proactively, turning to a team member and counselor to generate some practical advice.

Ultimately this simple step helped build teacher confidence, and in turn helped teachers build trusting relationships with their students. Students and teachers do spend advisory time attending to the important daily activities of school—grades, course selection, homework, and college scholarship applications. But more importantly, doors are opened to meaningful conversations around hopes, dreams, aspirations, barriers, and fears.

Taking advantage of the knowledge that educators in the district have developed through the relationships garnered through advisory and other means, Springdale chose to support each student through personal learning plans (PLP). Fully developed PLPs ask students to express themselves in their own voices—earning praise and recognition for their unique performances. The purpose of PLPs in Springdale is to provide a systematic way of guiding students to examine who they are by exploring their talents, interests, dreams, and aspirations.

Through this process of self-understanding, students become full partners in the learning process and are guided to set personal and learning goals; ask questions; explore how to find out more; and reflect on what they have learned in the process. District leadership established procedural aspects of this work, as well as working with the school leadership to vest all educators in the district in this process. Samples of PLPs are included in appendix B.

The student-led conference, a key component of the PLPs, provides a vehicle in which students are able to articulate, with supporting evidence, how they are progressing. During a student-led conference, students lead their adult supporters (parent, guardian, coach) through a thoughtful and thorough analysis of their progress to date, and commit to specific next steps for increased progress. Reflecting on their progress and articulating action plans builds ownership and leadership in students. Research on goal setting shows that committing to our goals in writing increases the likelihood of their accomplishment, and describing our commitment out loud provides an even greater chance of success.

It now seems strange to think that engaging students as partners in the process of setting goals, sharing progress, advising their teacher and their families about their hopes and dreams would be a difficult concept. We quickly learned that students are very capable of engaging in much more, and express their appreciation when they can contribute to their learning environment. The commitment to student-led conferences in Springdale was a driving force that could bring together all the elements of personalizing learning for all students. That commitment has resulted in all of the 22,000-plus students in the district conducting student-led (or student-involved in grades K through 2) conferences twice a year.

Advisory is one of those "sticky points" that schools often run up against, and the logistic challenges often shut down the effort before it really gets going. Administrators must adjust schedules to make time for this activity. They need to ensure advisors have time to learn and work together, and feel prepared for the activity. Advisors have to make a commitment to the process and the students, ensuring they can get to know each advisee academically and personally. They need to know what resources and referrals are available and when they are needed.

Goal setting with students is a foundational piece of the authentic implementation of personal learning plans and their subsequent use with student-led conferences. Students are not born with a fear of data. We must be strong ambassadors and protect our students from the sensation that data are negative influences. The use of data can be intimidating and frightful if there is a sense of retribution when the numbers do not look like we want them to. Numbers simply provide information. Unfortunately, numbers often become the fall-guy for the blame game and students are often victimized the aftermath of what summative data bring forward. The use of data is best served in an environment of continuous improvement.

We found it very helpful to look to experts in the field as we began the conversation about using data as part of the advisory, Personal Learning Plan (PLP) and Student-Led Conference (SLC) processes. We utilized the expertise and models of coaches to begin this initiative. It is very important that the students, families, and faculty understand how the data helps drive improvements for the future and does not simply reflect the past.

Students benefit when the data are recent and relevant. Data from writing rubrics that describe what proficient looks like, books that are leveled so students can recognize when they are moving from move level to another, and multiple opportunities to improve performance over time on skill-based assessments are excellent places to begin. Classes can set goals such as achieving 100 percent on an arithmetic fact timed test.

There is much to celebrate when improvements are noted from one timed test to another. Setting classroom or grade-level goals on percent of students passing their spelling test on the first try, or by meeting a goal for the number of books read in a quarter, can bring synergy to a class of students as they meet and celebrate their successes. Goal setting can be a fun and invigorating experience if the environment supports the use of data in a proactive and positive way.

Part III

IMPLICATIONS

I can make my parents comfortable when I am with them during student-led conferences. We have to be honest with them but I can take the stress out too. (Student 2018, Elmdale Elementary School)

Our story intentionally begins, and ends, with the voice of a student. Over the past five years I visited with students at every school in Springdale multiple times. On each visit, I asked them the same four simple questions:

- Can you define what it means to have voice and choice?
- What examples can you give me of voice and choice at school or at home?
- Why does it matter if you have a voice or are given choices?
- What suggestions would you give to the principal?

I heard amazing changes over those years as students developed confidence and skill in voicing their opinions.

During my first set of interviews, some students were hesitant to give their opinion. Some weren't sure what it meant to have a voice. The choices they did talk about were focused on home, and not so much at school. Some students said adults should make all the decisions—after all, they were the adults and knew best. Choices students did talk about focused on things like what to wear to school and when to do homework.

At the time I did not pursue the more in-depth questions since the conversations did not lend themselves to that end. To be fair and cautious about any conclusions, I initially chalked their limited responses up to the fact that I was a stranger and they were not familiar with me.

Skipping ahead to the final sets of interviews—the tone and content were significantly different. Real research conditions were not in effect—but the sensations were real. Elementary students at all schools spoke freely of the multiple choices they had—where to sit, with whom to sit, what to choose from the lunch line, what books to read, what specific writing assignments were available, and many others. The time set aside for the conversations sped by, often exceeding the time allotted because of all they were telling me.

When I asked them about their voice, they shared the various ways they could communicate through class meetings, principal advisory groups, and special leadership team options. In extended questioning about student-led conferences, students shared that they were very important, telling me things like, "My teacher doesn't know everything I want to tell my mother and dad about my school work." One young man admitted that he shared his weak math performance with his folks, telling them, "I haven't really been putting forth that much effort.—so, I guess I need to start paying attention."

Secondary students also shared with more breadth and enthusiasm than on the first visits. They recounted the importance of the advisory time to help them keep focused and get extra support when needed. They spoke about options they had for reading, writing assignments, alternative solutions in math class, and Socratic circles as a method to discuss issues in literature.

The impact of 1:1 technology was a major change in the conversation as well. Both elementary and secondary students expressed how the options available through the use of their Chromebooks were significant. Assignments are being posted so they can choose which of their assignments to complete first. There were more choices for students for acceleration as well as instructional support via the technology. K-12 technology and increased choice appear to go hand in hand.

Here is a major takeaway based on the voices of our students. We have students developing a growth mind-set, a major goal of personalization. Students with a growth mind-set can express their strengths and weaknesses, and create focused goals based on data. Students with a growth mind-set understand they are not passive vessels for knowledge; they have an active and responsible role to play in their own learning.

Listening to so many student voices helps us evolve as a learning system, but it also paints a compelling portrait of where we are. Springdale has undeniably shifted our culture toward personalization, and has developed structures and procedures to support and sustain that change. *Putting Students First* has become part of the way community members think about themselves, and it is hard to imagine any set of circumstances that might alter that perception.

In some ways our story is very simple. We teach the kids who show up in front of us every day. We study and talk about best practice models. We are always learning from and with others. We adapt everything, and never expect anything to go "according to plan." We want engaged students. We know deeper learning occurs when students have a voice and choice in the classroom.

These conversations gave me great hope that indeed the impact of transformed practice was taking root. We chip away at this process every day and continually seek to understand the myriad, and ever-changing, needs of the students in front of us. The one thing we can say with certainty is that our future will be different than our present.

But looking back there are some valuable lessons we've learned along the way that helped us on our journey. We have discovered that shaping a culture of putting students first rests on a few core beliefs, and these beliefs nurture innovation as much as they nurture sustainability. The beliefs are simple, yet difficult, to implement with honesty and integrity. They are not fancy or jargon-y, and might just work in other parts of life!

But we know they helped us put students first in Springdale. And we think they will help you too.

Chapter 8

Focus on Core Beliefs

Having voice and choice means I have more passion for my projects. When you have different options, you can express yourself in the way only you can. It makes me feel respected. (Student 2018, JO Kelly Middle School)

We are about to come to the end of our story but not the end of our journey toward personalization of learning. There will always be work to be done to match practice with student need. At the end of part I we briefly introduced the five core beliefs, beliefs that have been foundational to our success, the principles, and goals that hold steady through ever-changing conditions. Here we return to them and delve a little deeper into how they manifest themselves in Springdale.

REMEMBER WHAT'S IMPORTANT

Clear and consistent messages that are understood, and embraced, by all matter.

"Yes, we can do that" echoes across the Springdale halls and classrooms, and that attitude has everything to do with the ongoing success. In Springdale the message has been consistent, and the focus has always been on the student. Everyone looks at education as a moral imperative, and letting demographics determine destiny is just not an acceptable cultural norm.

It cannot be understated that having continuity in *leadership messages* matters. The ability to make sustainable change relies on a constant vision, mission, and plan for implementation. The leadership culture in Springdale has an outsize influence on sustaining a focused message. The long tenure of the superintendent (forty-plus years) and his belief in the power of public education are reflected in a community that weighs every action by its impact on students. Clearly the careful recruitment and hiring of staff sharing these values have contributed to the entrenchment of this message. You hear the common goals echoed in every corner of Springdale.

Schools in our district are very diverse. Some schools have 90 percent or more of their students on free and reduced lunch. Other schools have 80 percent of their children who are second language learners. Still other schools have very active parent organizations that can generate lots of resources for the school, while some other schools struggle to authentically engage families. We have some schools where most everyone can walk to school and other schools where everyone rides the bus.

All of these factors and more create unique conditions that must be respected when it comes to the nature and pace of change. In our experience, district-level personnel are best suited to create the conditions for change by providing the rationale for change, maintaining strong feedback communication channels, and providing resources and professional development support. Once the initiative has been "kicked off," the real magic begins as administrators and teachers use their best insight as to how change initiatives will work best for their students. In other words, the district sets the overall tone for what is important.

Many years ago, as a young parent, someone shared a small piece of advice that I still think about. "Say yes." What she meant was say YES to your children when they ask to do or explore or learn about things. NO only comes up when there are safety issues or the possibility of harm. That advice changed my life, and maybe changed the lives of my children. It's all about remembering what's important.

The respect for the "personality" of each school, each classroom, each group, and individual is entangled with the importance of core messages. *Remembering what's important* actually feeds the development of individuality for people and organizations because you can measure everything you want to do against the metric of a few, simple, unmoving principles.

EVERYONE MATTERS

Respecting every member of the community is good manners, and something we value in Springdale! But when you go beneath the surface and really work alongside students, teachers, families, and community members you begin to build and sustain things that were unimaginable on your own.

As a community that puts students first, respecting students and sharing leadership with them is a cultural norm. Taking responsibility for learning is part of that respect. In a sustainable system that respect needs to exist among all members of the community.

Caring for the teachers and educators who make this happen every day is also a cultural norm, and it is so enculturated in Springdale that people hardly notice it. You hear the stories of failure resulting from lack of support, infighting, and jealousy among staff far too often. *Teach them all* applies to every adult working or volunteering in Springdale as well. Professional knowledge is respected and nurtured, and teachers are empowered to manage their personalized learning journeys. As a core belief, allowing faculty to help set the agenda for change initiatives begins with presenting the case for why the change supports their students, and then allowing the scale-down process to take effect shaped by their insight.

Of course, a culture of respect doesn't develop or sustain by wishful thinking or good intentions alone. Mechanisms need to be built that reach out to the broader community and extend meaningful opportunities for involvement. In Springdale we built an innovative engagement program for the families of our immigrant students that resulted in honest collaboration with a group of typically marginalized individuals. The district offered ESL classes for adults that included free child care.

The classes were fun and engaging, co-taught by Springdale educators and immigrant community leaders. What made these classes so unique was their focus on learning about the community and school process while learning English. Participants even had the opportunity to role-play a student-led conference while preparing for their own experience with their child. Capping the experience off, parents got to put their new language skills to work as volunteers in classrooms.

EVERYTHING MATTERS

INFORMATION AND DATA MANAGEMENT

While it doesn't quite rise to level of a core strategy, flexible and efficient information management systems are really needed to support innovative practices. For example, the ability to innovate and experiment with grading policies is often limited by the capacity of a student information management system to handle alternate ways of reporting. The ability to disaggregate assessment results and focus on students who have been exposed to "new" practices for multiple years is also critical.

Springdale adopted the Schoology management system several years ago and found it eliminated many of our roadblocks and functioned as a tool to support innovation.

Springdale began this work as a Pre-K-12 initiative, and addressed both policy constraints and challenges to traditional practice from the onset. Doing everything at once is hard, messy, and often disorganized. But we believe it is the only path to lasting change.

For example, both in practice and policy, personalization in education is still thought of as a high school initiative in some places, and may be "rolled up" into the high school or "rolled down" to the lower levels. People debate how old students need to be before they can be partners in guiding their own learning.

Many efforts flourish *within* the policy constraints, stopping when they run into a state policy that runs counter to innovative programming Springdale's partnership with the state education department illustrates this back-and-forth tension. Shortly after receiving the Race to the Top District award in 2013, Springdale Schools applied for a "seat time" waiver from the State of Arkansas. This waiver (which was granted) was foundational to establishing the Don Tyson School of Innovation and the many other programs which have grown from it. Today the Arkansas Department of Education is a leader in the development of education policy, with a stated vision of transforming Arkansas to lead the nation in student-focused education. Since 2013, the State of Arkansas has been slowly building an enabling policy environment to support, and promote, transformative change in education.

The Arkansas General Assembly passed Act 601 in 2013, allowing "schools of innovation" to be established. This state statute permitted Arkansas schools and districts to apply for waivers of state policy in support of innovation. Additional legislation has followed. Act 1280 (2013) opened up new digital learning opportunities, resulting in an increasingly flexible use of time. For example, "snow days" are now known as "alternative learning days." Students and teachers can connect and work via technology rather than losing instructional days due to inclement weather.

Act 509 (2013) updated the Arkansas Charter School Act to more explicitly seek innovation in charter applications. This regulation also enabled flexibility and waivers in the application of state rules and regulations. Acts 1420 and 872 (2015) enabled districts to seek additional waivers, and to award credit based on demonstrated mastery rather than the traditional Carnegie Unit.

Today Arkansas is a leading model in developing policies that support personalization and competency education. Competency Works (iNACOL n.d.) considers Arkansas an advanced state, with comprehensive policy aligned and an active state role in building capacity in local school systems for competency education. Arkansas is also a member of the Innovation Lab Network, a group of states facilitated by the Council of Chief State School Officers acting to identify, test, and implement policies to support student-centered approaches to learning.

Within the district, we took the bold step of implementing student-led conferences *for all students, Pre-K-12*. As far as we could tell we were all alone in doing this, and we had many skeptics and critics telling us this approach could not work with the youngest students. But we thought if it mattered in the high school it would matter in the elementary school too, so we tried it out. Of course, the process looks different at different grade levels, but the essence of the experience is there for all.

WORK TOGETHER

"When you go out into the world, watch out for traffic, hold hands, and stick together" (Fulghum 2003). This notion of learning from and with others is really important in Springdale. Sharing our story through this book is a part of that learning, we know it will spark conversations that will lead us to ever deeper insights.

This belief really addresses a mind-set about change. The tradition of continuous learning is evident across the Springdale School District. But more than that—there is a culture that supported and embraced positive change where student welfare was concerned. As proverbial wisdom suggests, the driver to change starts with recognizing that there is a gap between current reality and desired reality. Professional learning teams at the district and building level were asking questions. Leading experts were consulted, their books were used as group book studies, professional development was provided to all faculty, and the leadership was willing to challenge the status quo.

Collaboration is a core belief. Staff point repeatedly to the value they find in collaborating through professional learning communities. Embedded in this idea of learning together is the invitation to experiment with new ways of doing things. Educators across the district frequently cite how empowered they feel in this area—to try new things and learn from both success and failure. The district leadership team consistently affirmed the message that individuals cannot perform effectively in silos or in isolation. Whether it is a teacher in the classroom, the building-level administrators, or the district leadership team, the concept of the professional learning community functioning as an ongoing system of collective inquiry is critical to the culture—in daily operations and when instituting major change.

The arrival of the Race to the Top District grant challenged us to implement multiple initiatives at once. We relied heavily on collaborative structures to enable implementation and support us through this period. Faculty from every school were invited to meetings where the specifics of the grant initiatives were shared and questions were addressed. Teachers on special assignment in specific curricular areas began working with teams of teachers to look at needed shifts in curriculum. Feedback loops were put into place with parents and faculty.

Schools benefit from formal and informal collaboration among educators. Curriculum development is an example of how collaboration and feedback can work. When designing curriculum documents, a team of specialists would generate the recommended course of action per grade level. Teachers would pilot the work and be given the opportunity to provide feedback—what worked, what did not. Tweaks and adjustments were made—formally and informally.

Formal feedback would be considered and changes would be published on the curriculum website page. Informal changes would occur within a school, within a specific grade, and may or may not be formally recognized. As long as the goal of meeting grade-level standards or meeting growth targets was on the radar, schools were given and deserved flexibility. Our experience suggests that micromanaging curriculum given the diverse needs across the district was not realistic or helpful. Accepting the notion that scaling down will occur within the expected outcomes of achievement generates a manageable system.

Of course, collaborative work does not happen organically. As leaders we provided a set of principles, norms, and time in the schedule to meet so that teachers, administrators, and school board members would have a successful experience. Our district participated in district-wide professional development on the PLC model in order to have a common vision, language, and practice around the concept of collaborative work environments.

CONNECT AND NETWORK

When we first started our journey, our district was part of a small group of like-minded educators scattered across the country. Through the USDOE we made fast friends with the twenty-five districts comprising the Race to the Top District cohort. We developed long-distance relationships with the schools that were part of the New England Network for Personalization and Performance. We clung to these friends because we needed their guidance and feedback as we explored new territory. We were all working to define, describe, and implement new ways of interacting with our students as we figured out this thing we were calling personalization.

But the landscape is shifting, driven by the rising numbers of administrators, teachers, families, and students engaged in personalized learning. Young students coming up in schools where voice and choice are the norm are expecting (and demanding!) the same culture in secondary schools. In the same way, the spread of personalization across schools has impacted, and shifted, policies across districts, states, and the nation.

Today I am happy to report that the policy support for personalization of learning is growing by leaps and bounds in Arkansas. The Arkansas Department of Education continues to shift toward innovation and the Arkansas General Assembly is creating legislation that removes barriers to personalization.

In January of 2013 the Arkansas Department of Education established the Office of Innovation for Education (OIE) at the University of Arkansas in Fayetteville. This research-focused office was intended to identify, cultivate, and support sustainable innovation across the state. A primary mechanism was the creation of a statewide learning community where we could learn together and realize shared goals for creating, refining, and sustaining innovative strategies that improve student learning and outcomes for every student. Since its establishment, the members of the OIE Innovation Learning Community have connected with national and international networks of educators and innovators.

Denise Airola, director of the OIE, explained,

> We collaborate and come alongside educator-innovators to help them navigate the process and to help them take informed risks on the road to transformation. We work to help schools manage that risk by connecting teachers and administrators who are doing similar work to enhance student and adult learning. These formal and informal connections support a growing network of innovators who learn from each other and support each other in implementing new ideas and designs for learning. The OIE now supports formal and informal networks of innovators at various stages of maturity. (Airola 2019)

Connecting through networks with a common focus accelerated our learning; there were fewer "reinventing the wheel" activities. Networks connected us to opportunities that were not open to us individually. For example, the Arkansas OIE network supported *A Learning Journey: Global Perspectives to Ignite Innovation in Education*. Springdale had the opportunity to send a team of teachers and administrators on a learning visit to New Zealand, selected for its notable success with students. The individuals who made that trip returned with new ideas and renewed enthusiasm for their efforts to create a more student-focused learning environment.

> The opportunity to visit seven New Zealand schools changed me forever. My lens for personalization of learning broadened in scope during that visit. When I left New Zealand, I had a renewed passion for developing innovative strategies to help personalized learning so all studentscan achieve at high levels. (Poage 2019)
>
> Our learning journey to New Zealand schools set a fire in me to pursue personalized learning, as well as altered my view and definition of personalization. (L. Johnson 2019)
>
> We started thinking deeply about student-centered learning after visiting schools in New Zealand. Schools operated differently in New Zealand. We saw deeper learning than we had experienced before. (Freeman 2019)

Of course, networked learning is a two-way street. Once you let go of the idea that there are "experts" with "solutions" out in the world you can honestly engage with peers and learn from one another. In 2017 Springdale educators were introduced to members of the ExcEL Leadership Academy (ExcEL Leadership Academy 2019) peer network located in Connecticut.

Our goals partly overlapped, with ExcEL focused on support and personalization for emergent bilinguals. ExcEL staff became very interested in our family literacy models, and have invited Springdale educators to Connecticut to work with schools on developing their own family programs. Networking is most effective when every member recognizes they have expertise to offer to the conversation.

Today the individuals comprising the Springdale education community are connected to a broad community of practice. We no longer feel isolated on the journey. We visit other schools and districts regularly, and we welcome visitors in our community. We encourage and support attendance at regional and national conferences for sharing and learning.

TRY NEW THINGS

Successful implementation of new programs requires planning, tailoring, tweaking, and adjusting any promising practice to fit the circumstances. Springdale practitioners were given leeway to modify practice within a framework of keeping the integrity of the practice. This was particularly evidenced in the district-wide introduction of advisory and student-led conferences. Practitioners should be given the freedom to adapt promising practices to meet the unique needs and demands of their school environment, while holding true to the purpose and goal of the initiative.

There are two big forces driving the adoption of new ideas and practices. One, scaling up, is the practice of spreading an initiative to multiple sites. We are generally pretty familiar with this concept and rely it on when we look for best practices to bring into our own district, schools, and classrooms. You might think of this as replication.

The other force is scaling down. Scaling down occurs when schools use the big ideas of an innovation but are expected to adapt the model to fit the needs of their school environment and/or comfort level. You might think of this as modification.

These two forces can be oppositional, or they can be complementary. We elect to balance them when trying new things.

We chose to implement student-led conferences in thirty schools in grades Pre-K through twelve. This was a scaling up practice, where we adopted something from outside the district and chose to replicate it at our schools. But it was successful because we balanced it with deliberate attention to scaling down. We gave each school the freedom to determine which grades they would start with, and what specific processes they would use. Schools created templates that made sense for their students and their families.

The models provided to us gave great suggestions—but schools were not bound by a strict set of rules. The maturity of students, space limitations, course selection requirements, and the graduation pathway all influenced how the student-led conferences were organized. The overarching goal for student-led conferences was met in each case. Students were sharing their data and academic goals in their own voices.

The advisory initiative was introduced, in part, to support the ability of a student to carry out the student-led conference, and is also a great example of how we tried new things. During advisory, caring supportive relationships are built, student data is shared and talked about, and students construct their goals.

The structure of advisory is very different from elementary to high school. In the elementary classroom, the advisory is more likely to be an integrated part of the classroom instruction as students review their reading scores, math assessments, and others with the outcome of constructing learning target goals. However, in the secondary school, dedicated time is provided for student cohorts paired with an adult advisor. Student advisory programs are now a common feature in Springdale schools, but they are not identical.

The goal of building an advisory where every student was meeting in small cohorts of students with a caring adult was the overarching goal. Schools were not given a strict protocol or structure for implementation. Each school was given the autonomy to build their own program based on a survey of student needs.

The CSSR helped us use the *Student Advisory Program Implementation Survey* and *Advisory Program Checklist* tools to accomplish the design—these tools are included in Appendices E and F respectively. School leaders experimented and listened to one another to uncover common pitfalls and how to avoid them. The result is a wide variety of homegrown programs reflecting the best fit in each school.

In practice, we try new things by scaling up and down at the same time. We scale up by piloting across multiple schools. We scale down by having each school or classroom adapt the model to fit their needs. This scaling allows all schools to ultimately meet the unique needs of their students.

Appendix A

Springdale School District Playbook

Springdale School District Playbook

Springdale School District Playbook. Springdale Public Schools, 2017.

Appendix A

Springdale School District Playbook
Table of Contents

Table of Contents	1
Introduction	2
Gameboard for Personalized Learning	3
Advisory/Primetime	4
Career Academies	5
Competency-Based Learning	6
Early Childhood	7
Family Literacy Program	8
Online Learning	9
Parent Involvement	10
Personal Learning Plans	11
Professional Learning Communities	12
Student-Led Conferences	13
Technology	14

Appendix A

MEMORANDUM
From the **Office of Race to the Top – District**

Introduction

Springdale School District has a history and tradition of best practice. Recently the Springdale School District has embraced the concept known as "personalization of learning." Personalization of learning occurs when educators create conditions that allow students to take ownership and responsibility for their learning.

The purpose of this *Playbook* is to highlight key practices that are the cornerstones to successful academic achievement within the framework of personalization of learning. Although there are other key practices not listed here, this is an introduction to those transformational practices linked to increased student agency. Additionally, it is anticipated that this *Playbook* will provide continuity of practice when new faculty members join the district.

It is expected that these practices will be modified or adjusted as we find better ways to meet the needs of our students. However, the fundamental vision and mission associated with each of the practices reflect the deeply rooted belief system of the district.

Special thanks to Dr. Megan Slocum, Ty Davis, Laura Bishop, Joanna Maddox, and Marsha Jones for contributions to the construction of the *Playbook*.

Special thanks to Superintendent Jim Rollins, Board members of the Springdale School District and faculty and administrators of the Springdale School District who made the transformational practices a reality!

Appendix A

Gameboard for Personalized Learning

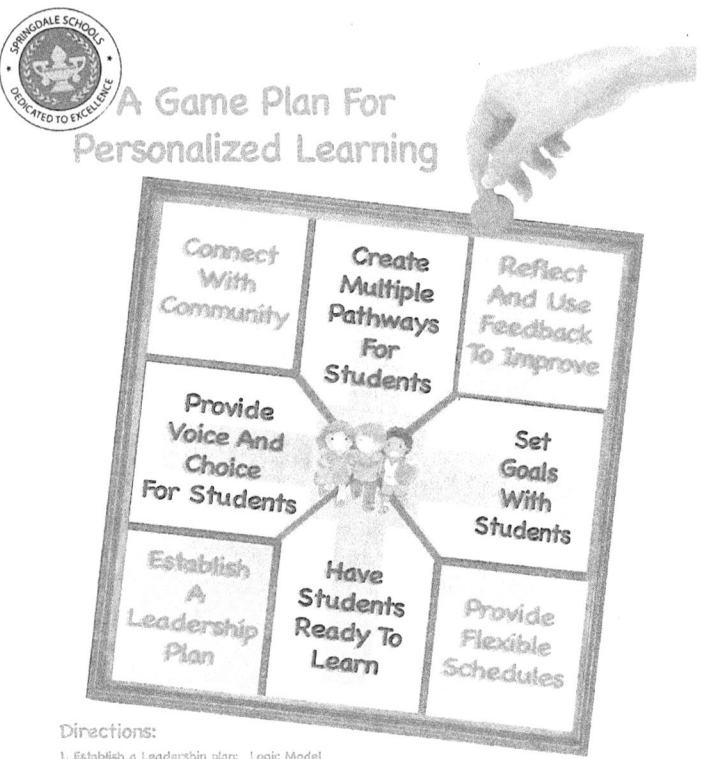

Directions:
1. Establish a Leadership plan: Logic Model
2. Have students ready to learn: PreK
3. Set goals with students: Personal Learning Plans/Student Led Conferences
4. Provide flexible schedules: Seat Time Waiver/ Revised Schedule
5. Provide voice and choice: Advisory/ Technology/ Highly Qualified Professional Development
6. Connect with Community: Parent Involvement
7. Create Multiple Pathways: Academies, School of Innovation
8. Reflect and use feedback to improve: Professional learning communities; coaching and evaluation

Advisory/Primetime

Vision: The vision of the advisory is to promote engagement between a teacher and a student in order to develop a relationship that is characterized by warmth, concern, openness and understanding; and to ensure that every student is known well by at least one adult. "Every student should be well known by at least one adult. Students should be able to rely on that adult to help learn from their experiences, comprehend physical changes and changing relations with family and peers and act on their behalf to marshal every school's and community resource needed for the student to succeed, and help fashion a promising vision of the future." (Carnegie Council on Adolescent Development, 1989. P. 40)

Mission: The mission of an advisory is to create meaningful relationships to facilitate each student's academic, career and personal success. It will help identify concerns and problems students may be having socially/academically. Advisory/Primetime helps builds a sense of community. It will also create a system for monitoring student progress.

Purpose: The Advisory/Primetime curriculum should be designed to meet the age appropriate needs of the students. At a minimum, the Advisory curriculum model should include:

1) A balance of activities among personal, academic and career focus areas. Topics such as understanding personal test data, developing study skills, grade and assignment checks, career exploration, resume writing, community service options, course selection, alignment of career pathways and course selection, learning styles, test-taking skills, and college exploration.
2) Activities for executive skill development including: communication skills, collaboration skills, problem solving skills and current issues of concern to students.
3) Time for students to listen to and talk with each other about concerns or issues on campus or in the community.
4) Celebrations of student successes.

Role of Student	Role of Educator	Role of Administrator
• Understand that the advisory program is part of the expected educational system where attendance and participation is required. • Utilize the tools and resources that assist students in tracking their grades, attendance, career goals and graduation requirements. • Participate in academic support systems that can increase state and local assessment scores. • Prepare for student-led conferences. • Utilize a Personal Learning Plan as a tool to support the activities within the advisory period.	• Support each advisees growth as a learner in all aspects of his or her school life. • Know each advisee academically and personally. • Make referrals to other professional support such as counselors as needed. • Consult with teachers, administrators and counseling staff regarding student needs. • Initiate contact with parents as needed. • Facilitate the academic and career planning for each advisor in collaboration with counselors. • Prepare students for life transitions including career development and post-secondary opportunities. • Provide academic support systems that can increase students' state and local assessment scores. • Facilitate student-led conferences. • Advise struggling students with information about support services and alert counselors and parents when need	• Provide time within the schedule for an advisory period (age-appropriate). • Provide professional development to advisors for role clarity in the advisory program. • Monitor the activities of the advisory program. • Review the advisory system and make changes as needed. • Ensure that each student has an advisor. • Provide a viable advisory curriculum in coordination with the faculty. • Communicate the work of the advisory program to parents. • Create a system where advisors, counselors, students and associated faculty members can communicate about the needs of the individual student.

Appendix A

Career Academies

Vision: To provide students multiple pathways to success through their secondary school experience including Career Academies.

Mission: To provide a variety of Career Academies, as defined by the National Standards of Practice for Career Academies, designed to prepare students for both college and career.

Purpose: The purpose of Career Academies include:
1) Small learning communities, including teachers, across several academic and technical subjects.
2) A cohort of students that follow a program of study.
3) College–prep sequential curriculum with a career theme (Note: A career theme can be any of the 16 found within the National Career Clusters taxonomy or variations on these themes.)
4) An Advisory Board that forges partnerships with employers, higher education institutions, and the community.
5) A two-, three-, or four-year experience ending in the senior year.
6) Opportunities for students to engage in post-secondary planning.
7) Dual credit options through articulation agreements as appropriate.
8) Development of a portfolio or capstone project as appropriate.
9) Opportunities for community involvement through guest speaking, real-world projects, shadowing, mentors, internships, community service, post-high school tours.
10) Use of data to evaluate student and academy progress toward meeting goals.

Role of Student	Role of Educator	Role of Administrator
• Have a purposeful reason for enrolling in the academy of choice. • Participate in the personal goal setting/exploration activities. • Be a positive representative that represents the school and the academy program well when working with community representatives. • Participate in the Advisory Board as appropriate. • Use academic and technical assessment data for self-reflection in a cycle of continuous improvement. • Create a culminating portfolio that is presented to academy board members, teachers, and administrators.	• Establish in writing the mission, goals and benchmarks for the academy. • Ensure a student-centered focus that seeks to raise, maintain and/or increase student motivation while in high school. • Ensure a rigorous curricular experience for all students. • Align academy to a CTE Pathway and credentialing if applicable. • Ensure equity in the enrollment that reflects the demographic mix of the school. • Meet credentialing requirements for their academy. • Facilitate the involvement of non-academy faculty as appropriate such as counselors, ESL instructors, special education instructors, etc. • Facilitate community involvement activities (mentoring, job shadowing, internships, real-world projects, guest speakers, post-high school tours, etc.). • Participate in appropriate professional development activities. • Create assessments that reflect student academic and technical learning.	• Program courses that support a clearly stated program of study including a definitive course sequence. • Ensure a selection process that is transparent and accessible to every student. • Ensure that 80% of the students in the academy classes are in the cohort of shared class time (minimum of 2 courses per grade). • Ensure common academy team planning time during the school day. • Advocate for the academy activities and garner public support. • Ensure appropriate funding to support the academy. • Ensure access to appropriate professional development for academy teachers.

Appendix A 99

Competency-Based Learning

Vision: An approach to ensure that all children are successful in developing the knowledge and skills they need for life by focusing on mastery of prioritized standards and personalized learning.

Mission: Through choice and resubmission opportunities, students attain mastery of the essential standards of learning of each subject area where academic achievement is separate from behaviors.

Purpose: The purpose of competency-based learning is to allow students the opportunity to demonstrate proficiency of competencies through choice in summative assessments. It will include personalized learning plans that may include advancement upon mastery. Competency-based learning allows students to demonstrate proficiency of competencies through choice in summative assessments. Formative assessments are used as feedback to teachers and to guide students toward goal of mastery (often ungraded or calculated as a very small percent of the overall grade). Opportunities for resubmission to reach mastery on summative assessments are offered after additional requirements have been met to show work toward meeting competency.

Role of Student	Role of Educator	Role of Administrator
• Ownership of own learning. • Master competencies while continuing to work on those not met while moving forward in the curriculum. • Choice in learning.	• Prioritize standards and create competencies that include application and creation of knowledge. • Explicit expectations communicated for reaching mastery. • Facilitator of learning. • Provide student choice in demonstrating competency mastery to personalize learning. • Provide timely, frequent feedback and differentiated support to guide students to mastery. • Support students who do not meet mastery with additional learning and resubmission opportunities. • Academic grades are separate from behavior/habits of mind.	• Provide professional development on competency-based learning. • Support teachers by allowing time to develop curriculum that is competency-based. • Provide technological resources for teachers to track student mastery and allow students and parents the ability to view students' progress at anytime. • Educate stakeholders on the benefits of competency-based learning.

Springdale School District Playbook 6

Appendix A

Early Childhood

Vision: To provide high quality early childhood education that prepares and equips students. The goal of the Pre-K program is to prepare students for the future in school and in life.

Mission: The Springdale Pre-K Program, in partnership with students, parents and community, will promote social, emotional, academic, and developmental skills so students are prepared for their future.

Purpose: The purpose of Early Childhood Centers is to:
1) Provide programs where children have access to learning environments where academics, social skills, and learning combine with fun to make each day an adventure.
2) Organize effective kindergarten transition plans for students and families.
3) Advocate for the wellness of students to support their health needs.

The Springdale Public School Pre-K program currently serves 1,380 students at 20 locations. All of the sites are quality approved through Arkansas' Better Beginnings. Each classroom has twenty (20) students enrolled and is instructed by a state licensed teacher and a paraprofessional that has their Child Development Associate Credential (CDA) or sixty (60) hours of college courses. Daily activities are planned according to Child Development Early Learning Standards, the adopted curriculum, D.I.G. (Develop, Inspire, Grow), Common Core Units and various other sources of activity ideas.

Role of Student	Role of Educator	Role of Administrator
<ul><li>Students will come to school with an open mindset to learn and engage in learning activities.</li><li>Students will engage in social activities to equip them with the skills to successfully transition into school.</li></ul>	<ul><li>Plan activities with the students' social, emotional, physical, and cognitive education in mind.</li><li>Collect data on the students to ensure indicators on Kindergarten Readiness checklist achieved.</li></ul>	<ul><li>Inform the community how to enroll in the early childhood program.</li><li>Equip teachers with the skills to prepare students to transition into the Springdale District School system.</li><li>Ensure teachers are trained on and develiver the proper assessments: Developmental Indicators for the Assessment of Learning, Kindergarten Readiness Indicators Checklist, Children's Progress Academic Assessment.</li></ul>

Springdale School District Playbook 7

Family Literacy Program

Vision: To support the academic achievement of English Learners and to connect diverse families with Springdale teachers and schools.

Mission: The Mission of the Springdale Family Literacy Program (SFLP) is to help parents and children achieve their greatest potential together through English Language development and literacy instruction while building the relationship between home and school.

Purpose: A unique, research-based parent engagement program for family members that have children from Pre-K to 7th grade come to their child's school four days per week for three hours per day for an adult class. The class includes time for Adult ESL instruction, time participating in their child's classroom and time learning about the American school system and connecting with the community. Free daycare is also provided to remove barriers for parents with young children to attend.

Role of Parent	Role of Educator	Role of Administrator
• Grow in your role as your child's first teacher. • Learn what and how your child learns in school, promote literacy with your child. • Learn how to speak, read, and write in English. • Learn about your child's teacher, classroom, and participate in their learning to assist with learning at home. • Learn about the American school system, establish relationships with members of the staff and engage in leadership roles in your child's school. • Connect to community resources.	Child's Teacher • Teach parents how children learn to promote academic achievement. • Teach parents how to participate in their child's education. • Foster meaningful engagement between parents and students. Adult's Teacher • Teach English Language Development lessons with a focus on communicating in real-life situations. • Provide parents the strategies necessary to meet the needs of their family and children during Parent Time. • Communicate with child's teacher and school administration.	• Recruit families to participate in the Family Literacy Program. • Effectively manage the Parent and Child Together Time (P.A.C.T.) by directly connecting students, parents, and teachers together so parents can see teachers modeling learning strategies that will give parents the tools that will help to support learning at home. • Connect with community members who can contribute to the program by providing education or resources to parent participants. • Build relationships with families to refine how the program can best meet their needs.

Online Learning

Vision: The online learning environment will create reflective learners that meet the needs of the diverse learners. Students will be equipped with the skills to be effective in the 21st century.

Mission: The mission of the virtual school is to create opportunities for all students to receive a quality education. Student will be provided with a flexible learning schedule to meet their diverse needs. The goal is to provide synchronous and asynchronous learning that aligns with the state curriculum.

Purpose: The purpose of the virtual school is to provide student-centered, self-directed and self-paced learning. The virtual school will provide access to learning to meeting the needs of the individual learner.

Definition of Online Learning: Online learning is the ability to provide instructional delivery methods to meet the needs of the student regardless of time and location that challenge them to excel academically.

Role of Student	Role of Educator	Role of Administrator
<ul><li>Students make a commitment to participate in daily learning.</li><li>Student will communicate with their teachers.</li><li>Student will follow timeline expectations.</li></ul>	<ul><li>Teachers need to excel in use of 21st century technologies.</li><li>Connect with students through various forms of multimedia to meet the needs of diverse learners.</li><li>Teachers will provide individual and group feedback to students to guide their learning experiences.</li><li>Teachers need to create opportunities to provide personalized learning experiences.</li><li>Teachers will assess students in formal and informal ways that show students processing of curriculum expectations. Teachers need to be organized and plan so student can succeed in a virtual environment.</li><li>Teachers will provide ongoing feedback of the online program to allow for changes and enhancements to be made.</li></ul>	<ul><li>Administrator will ensure that students and teachers are equipped with the proper technology to excel in the online learning environment.</li><li>Administrator will ensure that teachers are providing an opportunity for students to excel in the online learning environment.</li><li>Administrators will ensure that the online content is aligned with curriculum standards.</li></ul>

Appendix A 103

Parent Involvement

Vision: To provide opportunities for parents to be invested in their child's education to positively impact student success.

Mission: The mission of parent involvement is to provide parents with active forms of involvement to be invested in their child's education and future. Schools will survey the needs of students and their families to serve them. Schools will teach parents about the expectations they should have for their students. Expectations set a standard for student success and develop sense of vision. Springdale School District will make a special effort to engage parents in a variety of ways to meet their needs. Parents will be offered a variety of roles in well organized and long-lasting programs.

Purpose: The purpose of parent involvement is to develop and create a partnership between schools and families and to create a seamless environment where parents are given opportunities to be invested in their child's education. Parents need to understand how current decisions will relate to future outcomes of their student's success. Parents need to be invited to school improvement planning committees including advisory, parent teacher organizations and a variety of booster and other parent groups throughout the school. Ultimately, principals need to respond to the needs of families.

Role of Student	Role of Educator	Role of Administrator
• Students need to cooperate with their teachers to coordinator communications with their parents. • Students need to encourage their parents to check weekly newsletters, written communications, parent link, and school's social media. • Students need to show their parent weekly progress. Students need to be transparent with their parents about all the possible opportunities to be invested in their student's education. • Students need to understand why it is important for their parents to be involved.	• Teachers need to build excitement in the kids to get their parents interested in attending school functions. Students have to feel the enthusiasm from teachers so they will help recruit their parents to come to school functions. • Teachers need to ensure they provide an inviting classroom. • Teachers need to ensure that all communications home are translated in parents native languages written and oral. It is important to be specific with time, date, and purpose of meetings. Teachers needs to be specific about the grows and glows of their students education.	• It is important for principals to understand the "why" of parent involvement. When principals understand the "why" of parent involvement it helps direct specific actions. • Principals need to ask families specific questions about their children's education and future. • Principals need to teach parents how to connect and get support from home. Principals need to train parents how to develop expectations for their children. • Principals need to focus on the needs of families. Make decisions based off students and families needs. Provide resources and knowledge to the parents so they can help the students have success. Utilize social media to communicate with parents. Reduce and do not rely on emails to communicate with parents. Help parents prepare their students for transitions into next grades. • Principals need to help parents learn about opportunities outside of school to help their students.

Springdale School District Playbook 10

Personal Learning Plans

Vision: Each student will have an age-appropriate Personal Learning Plan that helps the student make connections between what he/she is learning at school and its relevance to the student's future (short-term and long-term).

Mission: Create opportunities through advisory activities so that each student can be engaged in the development and use of an age-appropriate Personal Learning Plan as he/she builds greater ownership of their current and future goals.

Purpose: The purpose of the Personal Learning Plan is to engage each student in establishing long-term and short-term goals, assessing his/her current status in their learning continuum, and to add value to school coursework as each student sets career goals. Personal Learning Plans develop in age-appropriate ways as each student progresses along the school continuum. The Personal Learning Plan is a tool to be used during student-led conferences.

Definition of a Personal Learning Plan: The Personal Learning Plan (PLP) is a planning document that guides and supports a student as they progress through their chosen school pathway. The student, with guidance from their school advisors, parents and community members, authors the PLP where applicable. Schools create structures, such as advisories, to support the development of the PLP including a review and rewrite of the PLP as appropriate to stay current with the students' personal goals and aspirations.

Role of Student	Role of Educator	Role of Administrator
<ul><li>Participate in the advisory activities that support the development of a Personal Learning Plan.</li><li>Utilize a template that supports an age-appropriate PLP including long-term and short-term goals as appropriate (academic and career).</li><li>Set age-appropriate personal long-term and short-term goals in academic, social and career areas.</li><li>Review, analyze and revise the PLP as needed or directed.</li><li>Utilize the PLP template within the context of the student-led conference as appropriate.</li><li>Use the PLP process as a guide in course selection from year to year.</li><li>Use the PLP process to determine areas in which additional remediation or acceleration is needed.</li><li>Use the PLP as a communication tool during the student-led conference and provide artifacts of work to share in the conference.</li></ul>	<ul><li>Provide the student time and opportunity within the advisory period to develop and maintain the Personal Learning Plan.</li><li>Provide data and other technical information needed in order for the student to have information required for the PLP.</li><li>Implement a set of activities (Advisory curriculum) that help support the student in goal setting (academic and/or career)</li><li>Assist students in setting specific (SMART) goals.</li><li>Assist the students in preparing to share their PLP during their student-led conference.</li></ul>	<ul><li>Provide professional development for staff in the purpose of and design of a Personal Learning Plan.</li><li>Ensure access to data so that students can analyze and make goals based on current data.</li><li>Provide appropriate protocols for delivering and managing the PLP program through an advisory model that is age-appropriate.</li><li>Create a parent engagement model that supports each student in long-term and short-term goal setting activities.</li><li>Support the PLP process with an appropriate curriculum to be used within the Advisory program.</li></ul>

Appendix A

Professional Learning Communities

Vision: Each educator in the Springdale School District will be an active participant in a Professional Learning Community based on the tenets established by Rick DuFour.

Mission: Each school site and district will create and support "collaborative teams whose members work interdependently to achieve common goals for which members are mutually accountable." (p. 11)

Purpose: The purpose of a Professional Learning Community is to:
1) Focus and commit to the learning for each student using an ongoing process in which educators work collaboratively in recurring cycles of collective inquiry and action research to achieve better results for the students they serve. (p. 11).
2) Establish goals for students (collectively and/or individually) that are specific, measurable, attainable, results oriented and time bound (SMART).
3) Focus on results and not activities.
4) Align building level goals with district goals.
5) Utilize common formative assessments as a tool for continuous improvement.
6) Use protocols for discussing data to ensure a safe environment for sharing data among faculty members.
7) Use data as a way to improve and change instructional practice as needed to improve student performance.

*The Springdale School District PLC process is grounded upon the work of Rick DuFour. All citations within the text are from the same source as noted at the bottom of the page.
DuFour, R., DuFour, R. Eaker, R., & Many, T. (2010) *Learning by Doing*. Bloomington, IN. Solution Tree

Role of Student	Role of Educator	Role of Administrator
• Attend school and participate in class activities so data can be gathered to drive instruction.	• Gather evidence of current levels of student learning. • Collaborate to develop strategies and ideas to build on strengths and address gaps in learning. • Implement strategies and ideas. • Collaboratively analyze the impact of changes in instructional practice looking to discover what was effective and what was not. • Maintain a cycle of continuous improvement and a focus on results by each member of the team.	• Ensure that time is available for the PLC process. • Ensure that the team functions in such a way as to carry out the mission of the PLC process. • Monitor and evaluate the activities and outcomes of the activities within the PLC process. • Attend PLC as needed or necessary to ensure that the purposes of the PLC are carried out. • Make course corrections as needed. • Ensure a guaranteed and viable curriculum. • Ensure access to formative assessment to monitor the learning of each student on a timely basis. • Create systems for intervention and enrichment for students.

Appendix A

Student-Led Conferences

Vision: To create an opportunity for students to showcase their learning to parents that allows parents to invest in their child's education.

Mission: To equip students with the skills necessary to be reflective while giving them the opportunity to have their parents join them in their personalize learning goals. To give students and parents a specific event to be reflective on the students educational goals and objectives.

Purpose: To help student, parents, and teachers be reflective on students learning to help them achieve educational goals. Student-led conferences equip students with skills to explain their learning and thinking. It allows students to track their progress and make decisions about their future with their parents.

Role of Student	Role of Educator	Role of Administrator
<ul><li>Students will produce a PLP which will be used as a communication tool during the student-led conference.</li><li>Students will rehearse the process in class prior to conference.</li><li>Students will advocate for themselves during the conference concerning if they feel they need their parent's help with study space or homework time.</li></ul>	<ul><li>Educators will designate a time to allow students to prepare for student-led conferences to showcase their learning.</li><li>Educators will provide resources and templates to students to allow student to showcase their work.</li><li>Educators will inform students the importance of having their parents attend student-led conferences.</li><li>Educators will communicate with parents on the value of attending student-led conferences.</li><li>Educator will be available during the SLC to support students.</li></ul>	<ul><li>Administrators will coordinate and create opportunities for parents and guardians to attend student-led conferences.</li><li>Administrators will educate teachers on the proper procedures of leading a student-led conference.</li><li>Administrators will create multiple opportunities for parents to attend student-led conferences.</li><li>Administrators need to educate parents on how to connect with their school to invest in their students' education.</li></ul>

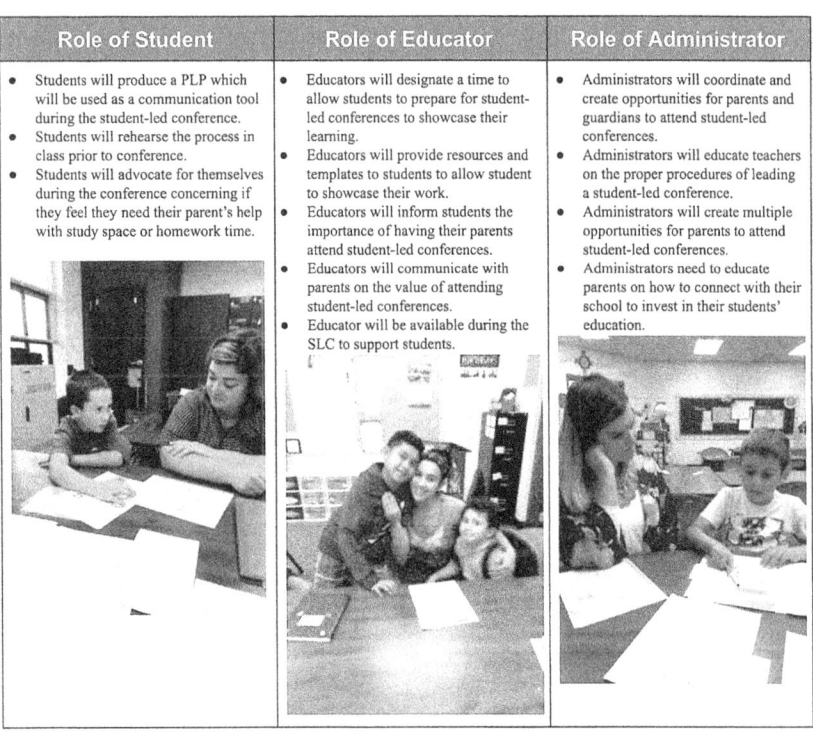

Appendix A 107

Technology

Vision: Use technology access and information resources to increase the quality of instruction and dramatically improve student achievement through a more personalized learning environment.

Mission: Technology in Springdale School District will be provided to each student in kindergarten through twelfth grade. Students will have access to information technology resources on a daily basis. Instructional alignment in the use of technology will reflect various levels of *SAMR within a 21st Century learning environment. *(Substitution, Augmentation, Modification and Redefinition). Technology will promote personalized learning experiences with a flexible learning environment. Technology will promote collaboration and meaningful collaboration.

Purpose: The purpose of technology in Springdale School District is to provide higher-order thinking of students in order to prepare them for a globally networked society and lifelong learning. Technology in Springdale School District will provide an infrastructure that supports and sustains the most current technologies to enable learners.

Role of Student	Role of Educator	Role of Administrator
• Students will employ technology to demonstrate learning in local and global collaborative environments. • Students will showcase their learning in a variety of digital formats to showcase their knowledge. • Students will create and present digital portfolios to showcase their learning. • Students will use digital etiquette when using digital technology.	• Teachers will facilitate students' access to current and relevant information and will use technology to differentiate learning. • Teachers will use technology for online communication with other communities, researchers, authors, scientists and international students and schools. • Teachers will attend professional development so they maximize and utilize their interactive whiteboards, computers, projectors, audio systems and webcams.	• Administrators will provide access and support to information and curriculum in and out of the classroom that connects curriculum areas and makes learning realistic while students achieve at the highest levels as defined by the Arkansas Department of Education. Develop and align a PK-12 technology curriculum aligned with Arkansas Department of Education standards.

Springdale School District Playbook 14

Appendix B

Personal Learning Plan Sample
Kindergarten

Appendix B

 Sonora Elementary K Personal Learning Plan

Student: _____ Year: _____ Teacher: _____

Literacy		
Fall Goal = 1148 Fall MAP Literacy Score:	Winter Goal = 1958 Winter MAP Literacy Score:	Spring Goal = 165 Spring MAP Literacy Score:
I am on/below/close grade level. (circle one)	I am on/below/close grade level. (circle one)	I am on/below/close grade level. (circle one)

Literacy Goal		
A B C D E F G H I J K L M N O P Q R S T U V W X Y Z		
Name Letters Make Sounds	Write Letters/Name	Read at Home (Parent Read Aloud and Book Bag Books)

Math		
Fall Goal = 148 Fall MAP Literacy Score:	Winter Goal = 159 Winter MAP Literacy Score:	Spring Goal = 166 Spring MAP Literacy Score:
I am on/below/close grade level. (circle one)	I am on/below/close grade level. (circle one)	I am on/below/close grade level. (circle one)

Math Goal		
100	SHAPES	$2 + 2 = 4$
Count to 25 (Fall) Count to 100 (Spring)	Name Shapes	Solve Math Problems

Behavior Goal			
Sit on carpet	Be a good friend	Do my work	Listen to follow directions

Signature of Student: _____ Date: _____
Signature of Teacher: _____ Date: _____
Signature of Parent/Guardian: _____ Date: _____

Personal Learning Plan Sample: Kindergarten. Sonora Elementary School, Springdale Public Schools.

Appendix C

Personal Learning Plan Sample
Grade 1

Appendix C

Sonora Elementary 1st Grade Personal Learning Plan

Student: _____ Year: _____ Teacher: _____

Literacy		
Fall Goal = 168 Fall MAP Literacy Score: _____	Fall Goal = 179 Fall MAP Literacy Score: _____	Fall Goal = 185 Fall MAP Literacy Score: _____
I am on/below/close grade level. (circle one)	I am on/below/close grade level. (circle one)	I am on/below/close grade level. (circle one)
My Reading Action Plan (How will I reach my goal?)		
Ask and answer questions while I read.	Read Sight Words (Current # ____)	Read at Home
My Writing Action Plan (How will I reach my goal?)		
Use uppercase letters, lowercase letters, and punctuation correctly.	Produce simple and compound sentences	Write to tell a story.
Math		
Fall Goal = 169 Fall MAP Literacy Score: _____	Fall Goal = 181 Fall MAP Literacy Score: _____	Fall Goal = 188 Fall MAP Literacy Score: _____
I am on/below/close grade level. (circle one)	I am on/below/close grade level. (circle one)	I am on/below/close grade level. (circle one)

ST Math Progress

25%	50%	75%	100%

My Math Action Plan (How will I reach my goal?)		
Count to 120 from any number.	Know addition and subtraction facts to 10	Solve + and -math problems

Signature of Student: _____ Date: _____
Signature of Teacher: _____ Date: _____
Signature of Parent/Guardian: _____ Date: _____

Personal Learning Plan Sample: Grade 1. Sonora Elementary School, Springdale Public Schools.

Appendix D

Personal Learning Plan Sample
Grade 2

Sonora Elementary 2nd Grade Personal Learning Plan

Student: _____ Year: _____ Teacher: _____

Literacy		
Fall Goal = 183 Fall MAP Literacy Score:	Winter Goal = 192 Winter MAP Literacy Score:	Spring Goal = 197 Spring MAP Literacy Score:
I am on/below/close grade level. (circle one)	I am on/below/close grade level. (circle one)	I am on/below/close grade level. (circle one)
My Reading Action Plan (How will I reach my goal?)		
Ask and answer questions while I read.	Read with accuracy & fluency.	Read at Home.
My Writing Action Plan (How will I reach my goal?)		
Use uppercase letters, lowercase letters, and punctuation correctly	Produce simple and compound sentences	Write to tell a story
Math		
Fall Goal = 184 Fall MAP Literacy Score:	Winter Goal = 193 Winter MAP Literacy Score:	Spring Goal = 199 Spring MAP Literacy Score:
I am on/below/close grade level. (circle one)	I am on/below/close grade level. (circle one)	I am on/below/close grade level. (circle one)
My Math Action Plan (How will I reach my goal?)		
Count to 1000.	Fluently add/subtract to 20 using mental images.	Explain why addition and subtraction problems work.

Signature of Student: _____ Date: _____
Signature of Teacher: _____ Date: _____
Signature of Parent/Guardian: _____ Date: _____

Personal Learning Plan Sample: Grade 2. Sonora Elementary School, Springdale Public Schools.

Appendix E

Student Advisory Program Implementation Survey

STUDENT ADVISORY PROGRAM IMPLEMENTATION SURVEY

Directions: Read each item and rate where your school currently stands regarding the ADVISORY PROGRAM 1=disagree, 5=agree. Add totals for the subset in the small box under each section.

Set #1: THE PLANNING	
The school did a good job of explaining what an advisory program was to all incoming freshmen prior to arriving for the start of the school year.	1 2 3 4 5

Total: ☐

Set #2: THE PURPOSE	
Your advisor clearly explained the purpose of the advisory program on day one, and talked about the social, emotional, and academic strengths of the program.	1 2 3 4 5
Your advisor supports the power of an advisory program, understands its importance, and does an effective job in creating a warm and welcoming environment that allows for conversation, trust, and relationship building.	1 2 3 4 5
If someone came up to you out of the blue and asked you to explain what an advisory program was, and how it improves student success, could you do it?	1 2 3 4 5

Total: ☐

Set #3: THE ORGANIZATION	
The advisory period meets enough times throughout the month for effective relationship building to take place.	1 2 3 4 5
The advisory period is long enough (when it does meet) for students and their advisor to share ideas, engage in powerful conversation, and build a solid relationship.	1 2 3 4 5
In your own advisory class, you see the "big picture" that each advisory period is leading to. In other words, your advisor plans activities and conversations that align together, have clear outcomes, and lead into future topics.	1 2 3 4 5

Total: ☐

Student Advisory Program Implementation Survey. Center for Secondary School Redesign, Inc., 2009.

Set #4: THE CONTENT	
You engage in activities and discussions that have clear objectives, examine both academic and social issues, and challenge students to examine real-life topics.	1 2 3 4 5
The advisor suggests topics and develops activities that allow students to openly discuss issues, think at a higher level, and share concepts and ideas with fellow classmates.	1 2 3 4 5
Overall, the feel to the advisory period is different than all of your other academic classes. It is more informal, and has a personalized focus.	1 2 3 4 5

Total:

Set #5: THE ASSESSMENT	
Your advisor does a good job of involving all students in your class, and encourages everyone to share opinions, ideas, and concerns.	1 2 3 4 5
Each advisory period is structured, and has an adult advisor who engages the students and sets expectations for everyone.	1 2 3 4 5
The advisor does a good job of holding all students accountable for their actions during the period.	1 2 3 4 5

Total:

Set #6: THE PERSONALIZATION	
Your advisor is someone in the school that you trust and would approach to talk with during stressful times or if a problem came up.	1 2 3 4 5
Your advisor knows who you are, can identify your strengths, and understands you as a young adult.	1 2 3 4 5
You have developed a strong relationship with your advisor throughout the school year.	1 2 3 4 5

Total:

Set #7: THE OVERALL PROGRAM EVALUATION	
The advisory program has helped make your transition into the high school a pleasant one.	1 2 3 4 5
You would suggest that all freshman take part in an advisory program.	1 2 3 4 5
You see the power of advisory, and would like it to be a part of your day-to-day schedule for the remaining three years of high school.	1 2 3 4 5

Total:

Appendix E

Advisory Implementation Survey

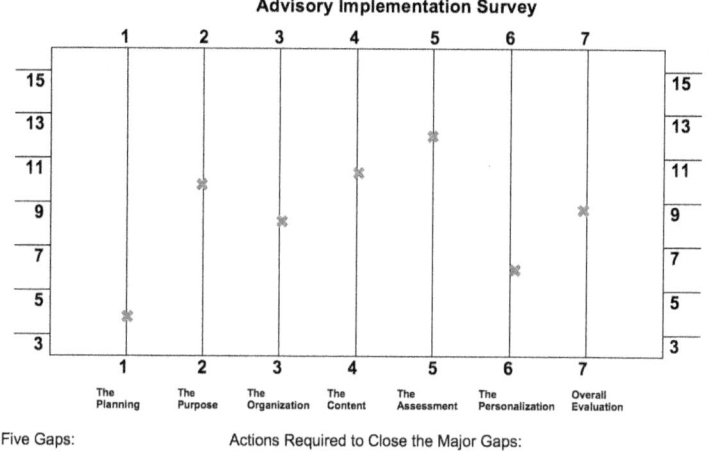

Top Five Gaps:
- _____
- _____
- _____
- _____
- _____

Actions Required to Close the Major Gaps:
1. _____
2. _____
3. _____

Appendix F

Advisory Program Implementation Checklist

Advisory Program Implementation Checklist

Purpose	**Yes**	**No**

The advisory purpose statement is written and reflects commonly held beliefs of the school community concerning student needs.

The advisory purpose statement is directly related to student and school community needs.

The advisory purpose is easily understood and embraced by all stakeholders, especially students.

The advisory purpose statement will have a positive emotional impact on those who read it.

The advisory program brings the purpose statement to life, in a way that results in meaningful and long-lasting changes, versus just tweaks.

The statement reflects an approach to meeting student needs that can't be met in any other way that is more efficient or effective.

Organization	**Yes**	**No**

The advisory organization elements address all aspects of the advisory purpose.

The organization reflects a deep focus on what must be done—it is very targeted in facilitating the accomplishment of the advisory goals.

All elements of the organization design are "intentional," that is, each element relates to achieving the advisory purpose.

The advisory organizational design leverages school strengths.

The knowledge and skill development requirements associated with each element are clear and can be addressed effectively.

Content	**Yes**	**No**

The advisory program content is easily understood and embraced by all stakeholders, especially students

The content reflects a deep focus on what must be done—it is very targeted for facilitating the accomplishment of the advisory purpose.

(Continued)

Advisory Program Implementation Checklist (*Continued*)

The content design is not just pie in the sky—it is doable.
All elements of the content are "intentional," that is, each element relates to achieving advisory goals.
There exists a rationale for what content was left out of the plan.
The design leverages your strengths as a school.
The path to content design implementation is clear.
The knowledge and skill development requirements associated with each content element are clear and can be addressed effectively.
The knowledge and skill development requirements necessary to make the content come alive and fully engage students are clear and can be addressed effectively.
The knowledge and skill requirements to effectively engage students and personalize the advisory experience, exclusive of content, are clear and can be addressed effectively.

Assessment Yes No

The advisory assessment design makes sense to all stakeholders.
The assessment elements support all aspects of advisory purpose.
The assessment design is not just pie in the sky—it is doable.
The assessment design is practical, that is, it is neither unwieldy nor too costly to implement and sustain.
All elements of assessment design are "intentional," that is, you can provide a meaningful rationale for each element as it relates to achieving advisory goals.
The design leverages school strengths with regard to assessment methodologies currently being employed.
The knowledge and skill development requirements associated with each assessment element are clear and can be addressed effectively.

Leadership and Professional Development Yes No

The advisory leadership team has built and maintains a vision, direction, and focus for the advisory program including everyone's role in that vision
Student needs are put ahead of adult needs
Leaders have an accurate pulse on what is going on, that is, individual or group needs and concerns and professional development are designed to address those needs and concerns
Leadership team members are encouraged to speak freely and express new ideas

Center for Secondary School Redesign, Inc., 2009.

Bibliography

Airola, Denise, interview by Marsha Jones. 2019. Springdale Partner Interviews.
Anonymous, interview by Marsha Jones. 2014. Student interviews on personalization.
Arkansas Online News. 2019. "Springdale Students Bond Over Drone Education." Arkansas Online News, May 17.
Avery, Laureen, and Jason Cervone. 2017. Evaluation Report for the Springdale Public Schools: July 2016–June 2017. Project Evaluation Report, Los Angeles, CA: UCLA Center X.
Bramante, Fred, and Rose Colby. 2012. *Off the Clock: Moving Education from Time to Competency*. Thousand Oaks, CA: Sage.
Bray, Barbara, and Kathleen McClaskey. 2014. Personalization vs Differentiation vs Individualization (PDI) Chart v3. Accessed August 2019. https://kathleenmccl askey.com/personalization-vs-differentiation-vs-individualization-chart/.
Childress, Maribel, interview by Marsha Jones. 2019. Springdale Administrator Interviews.
DiMartino, Joseph, interview by Dr. Marsha Jones. 2019. Springdale Partner Interviews.
Dufour, Richard, and Robert Eaker. 1998. *Professional Learning Communities at Work: Best Practices for Enhancing Student Achievement*. Bloomington, IN: Solution Tree.
Dufour, Richard, and Robert J. Marzano. 2011. *Leaders of Learning: How District, School, and Classroom Leaders Improve Student Achievement*. Bloomington, IN: Solution Tree.
Edmonds, Ronald R. 1979. "Effective Schools for the Urban Poor." *Educational Leadership* 37 15–24.
ExcEL Leadership Academy. 2019. ExcEL Leadership Academy. https://www.excel-leadershipacademy.org/.
Fisher, Douglas, and Nancy Frey. 2014. *Better Learning Through Structured Teaching: A Framework for the Graduaal Release of Responsibility*. Alexandria, VA: ASCD.

Freeman, Annette, interview by Marsha Jones. 2019. Springdale Administrator Interviews.

Fulghum, Robert. 2003. *All I Really Need to Know I Learned in Kindergarten.* New York: Ballantine Books.

iNACOL. n.d. Competency Works. Accessed 2019. https://www.competencyworks.org/.

Johnson, Kari, interview by Marsha Jones. 2019. Springdale Teacher Interviews.

Johnson, Leigh, interview by Marsha Jones. 2019. Springdale Teacher Interviews.

Jones, Marsha. 2019. "Unpublished."

Lezotte, Lawrence W., and Kathleen McKee Snyder. 2010. *What Effective Schools Do: Re-Envisioning the Correlates.* Bloomington, IN: Solution Tree.

Poage, Shelly, interview by Marsha Jones. 2019. Springdale Administrator Interviews.

Ray, Joshua, interview by Dr. Marsha Jones. 2019. Principal, East Pointe Elementary School, Greenwood, AR.

Rollins, Dr. Jim. 2017. "Speech to First Graduating Class, Don Tyson School of Innovation." Springdale, AR.

Rollins, Jim. 2019. "Speech to Archer HS Graduating Class." Springdale, AR, May 17.

Rollins, Jim, interview by Marsha Jones. 2019. Springdale Superintendent Interview.

Sinek, Simon. 2009. *Start With Why: How Great Leaders Inspire Everyone to Take Action.* New York: Penguin.

Sizer, Theodore R. 1984. *Horace's Compromise.* New York: Houghton Mifflin.

———. 2013. *The New American High School.* San Francisco, CA: Jossey-Bass.

Springdale Public Schools. 2014. "Race to the Top – District Project Logic Model." Logic Model.

———. 2018. Springdale Annual Report to the Public 2017–18. Springdale, AR: Springdale Public Schools.

———. 2016. Springdale Curriculum. Accessed September 2, 2019. https://sites.google.com/sdale.org/curriculum.

———. 2017. Springdale Game Plan for Personalized Learning. Guidebook, Springdale, AR: Springdale Public Schools.

Stewman, Regina, interview by Marsha Jones. 2019. Springdale Administrator Interviews.

Sugg, Jennifer, interview by Marsha Jones. 2019. Springdale Staff Interviews.

Tomlinson, C.A. 1999. *The Differentiated Classroom.* Arlington, VA: ASCD.

Wiggins, Grant, and Jay McTighe. 2005. *Understanding by Design.* Alexandria, VA: ASCD.

Yamaguchi, Ryoko, Laureen Avery, Jason Cervone, Lisa DiMartino, and Adam Hall. 2017. *Adaptive Implementation: Navigating the School Improvement Landscape.* Lanham, MD: Rowman & Littlefield.

About the Authors

Marsha Jones is a forty-plus-year veteran of education with a breadth of experiences in the classroom and at the district level. Personalizing education for each student has been her life's ambition, whether working in the elementary classroom, with special needs children, high school students, or currently with graduate students.

Laureen Avery leads the work of UCLA's Center X efforts in the Northeastern United States, and has more than thirty years of experience in K-12 public education as a researcher and practitioner. Avery developed and leads whole school improvement programs focused on improving outcomes for English learners and at-risk students.

Joseph DiMartino is founder and president of the CSSR, a nationally recognized provider of technical assistance to districts and schools that are personalizing learning for adolescents. For the past two decades, CSSR has been a strong advocate for including student voice and choice in their education. DiMartino has been named the national expert on high school redesign by ASCD and received the Distinguished Service to Education Award by NASSP.

www.ingramcontent.com/pod-product-compliance
Lightning Source LLC
Chambersburg PA
CBHW051814230426
43672CB00012B/2734